YOUR LIFE
IN THE
HOLY SPIRIT

What Every Catholic
Needs to Know and
Experience

YOUR LIFE
IN THE
HOLY SPIRIT

What Every Catholic
Needs to Know and
Experience

Alan Schreck

Published by The Word Among Us Press
7115 Guilford Drive, Suite 100
Frederick, Maryland 21704
www.wau.org

18 17 16 15 14   6 7 8 9 10

ISBN: 978-1-59325-105-5

Scripture texts used in this work are taken from the Revised Standard Version Bible:
Catholic Edition, copyright © 1965 and 1966 by the Division of Christian Education
of the National Council of the Churches of Christ in the USA.
All rights reserved. Used with permission.
Cover design by Adam Moroschan

Nihil obstat: Reverend James Dunfee
                Censor Librorum
Imprimatur: Most Reverend Gilbert I. Sheldon
                Bishop of Steubenville
                June 19, 1995

Library of Congress Cataloging-in-Publication Data
Schreck, Alan.
Your life in the Holy Spirit : what every Catholic needs to know and experience /
Alan Schreck. -- Rev. ed.
    p. cm.
Rev. ed. of: Hearts aflame. c1995.
Includes bibliographical references.
ISBN 978-1-59325-105-5 (alk. paper)
1. Spirituality--Catholic Church. 2. Holy Spirit. 3. Catholic Church--Doctrines.
I. Schreck, Alan. Hearts aflame. II. Title.
BX2350.65.S37 2007
231'.3--dc22
                                                        2007020982

To all the holy priests
who have taught me
the ways of the Spirit,
especially
Fr. George Montague, SM
Fr. Edward O'Connor, CSC
Fr. Daniel Sinisi, TOR
Fr. Augustine Donegan, TOR
and my pastors in the
Servants of Christ the King Parish

Contents

Acknowledgments

I would like to give thanks for all the assistance I received in writing this book and for all those places in my life where the Holy Spirit has been active and I have learned his ways: my family, parishes, Catholic schools (especially Franciscan University of Steubenville, where I have taught for the last thirty years), and charismatic prayer groups and covenant communities. I am especially thankful to the Lord for my wife, Nancy, with whom I have shared all joys and adventures of life in Christ and his Spirit for twenty-five years at this writing.

Alan Schreck
June 15, 2007

> And my God will supply every need of yours according to his riches in glory in Christ Jesus. To our God and Father be glory for ever and ever. Amen.
> **—Philippians 4:19-20**

Introduction

When I was in college, someone gave me a small pocket edition of the New Testament. The translation was not the best, but one day I came across something in it that stopped me in my tracks. It read, "Does your life in Christ make you strong? Does his love comfort you? Do you have fellowship with the Holy Spirit?" I had to admit that for me, the answer at the time was no—and I certainly had no idea what it meant to "have fellowship with the Holy Spirit."

Like most Catholics, I knew that the Holy Spirit was the third person of the blessed Trinity. I knew that I had received the Holy Spirit in my baptism, and more fully in the Sacrament of Confirmation. Although I accepted what the church taught about the Holy Spirit, that teaching didn't make too much difference in the way I lived. I rarely thought about it.

I believe that many Christians view the Holy Spirit in much the same way. He seems mysterious and unimportant to their faith and everyday lives. Some Christians even consider people who focus on the Holy Spirit and his activity to be unbalanced, emotional enthusiasts who are on the fringe of the church.

Yet if one were to ask these Christians, "Is the Holy Spirit important?" they would likely respond, "Of course. The Holy Spirit is God!"

How do we explain this paradox? I think that while most Christians have some clear idea of the person and work of the Father and the Son, and thus find it possible to have a relationship with them, the same is not true of the Holy Spirit. The typical Christian's notion of the Holy Spirit and his work is often vague and muddled.

This book is intended to help people come to a better, clearer understanding of the Holy Spirit and to help them discover the difference the Holy Spirit can make in their lives. I hope to "introduce" or "re-introduce" you to the Holy Spirit, so that you might come to know the Spirit, or know him better, and grow in your fellowship with him.

The First Step

The first step is to realize that the Holy Spirit is at the "heart" of God and of the gospel, the "good news" of Jesus Christ. Of course, the Bible contains plenty of good news that Christians can benefit from and rejoice in: the revelation of God's love, his law, his wisdom, and the stories and testimonies of the faith of God's people through the centuries. All of this and much more comprise the good news of biblical revelation.

But what is at the heart of the Bible and the gospel of Christ? It is God's revelation of himself! The height of Christian revelation is this:

- God is the Father, the source of all good, who created you, loves you unconditionally, and wants you to know him and relate to him as "Abba," your dear and beloved Father;
- God, in the person of Jesus Christ, is the Word or Son of the Father, who became human to reveal the loving Father and to show the Father's love by his words and deeds—especially by dying to atone for our sin, that we might live eternally with God in the joy of heaven;
- God is the Holy Spirit, through whom God lives within us, revealing to us the truth about the Father and Jesus and all the truths they desire us to know, and empowering us to live and to follow the way of Jesus and the Father, by which we receive the gift of eternal life.

The heart of the gospel is the truth about God himself. The truth about God is that he is one God in three persons: Father, Son, and Holy Spirit. Christianity declares that to be fully alive is to be "reborn" by the gift of Jesus Christ through faith and baptism, and from there to grow in knowledge and love of God—the Father, the Son, and the Holy Spirit. As St. Cyril of Jerusalem put it,

> Now real and true life is none other than the Father, who is the fountain of life and who pours forth his heavenly gifts on all creatures through the Son in the Holy Spirit, and the good things of eternal life are faithfully promised to us men also, because of his love for us.[1]

The importance of discovering the full truth about God, with the Holy Spirit at the heart of the mystery of the Trinity, was accentuated by Pope John Paul II in his apostolic letter *Tertio Millennio Adveniente* (As the Third Millennium Draws Near). To prepare for the celebration of the two-thousand–year anniversary of Christianity, the pope called upon Catholics to ponder "the mystery of the Trinity and the continuation of the Son's mission in the mission of the Holy Spirit."[2] Concerning the Holy Spirit, he wrote,

> The Church cannot prepare for the new millennium "in any other way than *in the Holy Spirit*. What was accomplished by the power of the Holy Spirit 'in the fullness of time' can only through the Spirit's power now emerge from the memory of the Church."
>
> The Spirit, in fact, makes present in the Church of every time and place the unique revelation brought by Christ to humanity, making it alive and active in the soul of each individual. . . .
>
> In our own day too, the Spirit is *the principal agent of the new evangelization*. Hence it will be important

to gain a renewed appreciation of the Spirit as the One who builds the kingdom of God within the course of history and prepares its full manifestation in Jesus Christ, stirring people's hearts and quickening in our world the seeds of the full salvation that will come at the end of time.[3]

Obviously, any form of Christianity that omits or neglects the Holy Spirit (or any member of the Trinity), or that ignores the importance of a relationship with him, is sorely deficient. Christian tradition affirms that the persons of the blessed Trinity are perfectly equal and one, though not identical. The Holy Spirit is at the heart of God. As St. Augustine said, the Spirit is the very love binding together the Father and the Son in perfect unity. He is also the love binding us to God (see 1 John 4:13) and to one another in God (see 1 Corinthians 12:12-13; Ephesians 4:3-4). Love is an expression of the heart, and the Holy Spirit is the deepest, fullest expression of God's "heart"—of God's love (see Romans 5:5). To encounter the Holy Spirit is to encounter God, for "God is love" (1 John 4:8).

As the letter to the Hebrews puts it, "Our God is a consuming fire" (Hebrews 12:29)—a fire of holiness and purity, and a fire of consuming love. It is little wonder that when the Holy Spirit first descended on the disciples of Jesus, he was described by St. Luke as "tongues of fire" resting upon the apostles (Acts 2:3). Their lives and hearts were set aflame with the living presence of God, coming to dwell within them (see 1 Corinthians 3:16; 6:19). Only then was the church of Christ born.

A gospel without the Holy Spirit at the heart is not the gospel of Christ. A Christian life without the Holy Spirit at the heart is not fully Christian. This movement into the fullness of life can happen only as the Holy Spirit takes his rightful place in our hearts. And so every person, every Christian, can benefit from coming to discover (or to discover more fully) the person of the Holy Spirit and his work. We can rejoice in the new relationship we have with God and with each other in the Holy Spirit. May we come to thank God even more fully for his infinite love and wisdom in revealing himself and giving himself to us in his Holy Spirit!

CHAPTER ONE

Who Is the Holy Spirit?

Many articles and books have been written about the Holy Spirit as the invisible, shy, mysterious, or even missing person of the blessed Trinity. This is not surprising if we consider the names and images for the Spirit of God that we find in the Bible.

"Spirit," for example, comes from the Hebrew *ruah*, which is literally translated "breath" or "wind." Invisible and free but also life giving, alternately gentle and serene, or powerful and howling—all this is implied in this meaning of "spirit." "Spirit" is appropriately chosen as a name for the third person of God. We do not see the Spirit, but he is life. His presence and voice can be as gentle as a spring breeze or as forceful as a hurricane. He is the *Holy* Spirit, because he is God—the one who *is* holy—totally unlike and infinitely above all else.

The very word "spirit" makes the Holy Spirit difficult to picture in our minds. Other images of the Spirit in Scripture are somewhat more concrete, and each one highlights different truths about him.[1]

The Holy Spirit is portrayed as *living water* flowing from the believer's heart (see John 7:38-39; Ezekiel 47:1-12; Isaiah 44:3-4; 55:1; 58:11; Revelation 22:1-2). This image reveals the Spirit as God's life-giving refreshment, cleansing and healing.

The Holy Spirit is represented as a *dove* that descended upon Jesus (see Matthew 3:16; Mark 1:10, 3:33; John 1:32). This image evokes the memory of God's covenant with Noah and represents the beginning of a new covenant that surpasses the old. The dove is a sign of the peace and purity of the Holy Spirit, which he gives to those who receive him.

The Spirit is presented as the *tongues of fire* at Pentecost (see Acts 2:3). He is also the *radiant, purifying fire* manifested in the prophets—among them, Elijah, John the Baptist, and, ultimately, Jesus, who came to "baptize you with the Holy Spirit and with fire" (Luke 3:16). Jesus said, "I came to cast fire upon the earth; and would that it were already kindled" (Luke 12:49).

The Holy Spirit is the presence of God displayed in the *cloud* of glory overshadowing Moses on Mount Sinai (see Exodus 24:15-18). The cloud also appeared at the tent of meeting (see Exodus 33:9-10); it led the Jews wandering in the desert (see Exodus 40:36-38); it was with Solomon as he dedicated the temple (see 1 Kings 8:10-12). This image of a cloud or overshadowing presence symbolizes the fact that the Holy Spirit is God's presence with his people. We see the image of the cloud in the New Testament, too. The Holy Spirit "overshadowed" the Virgin Mary so that she could conceive and give birth to Jesus (see Luke 1:35). Later, the Spirit's presence became visible in the form of the cloud that overshadowed Jesus at the mount of the transfiguration (see Luke 9:34-35) and at his ascension into heaven (see Acts 1:9).

The Holy Spirit is the preeminent and priceless *gift* of God. St. Thomas Aquinas taught in his *Summa Theologiae* that apart from the proper name, "Holy Spirit," the names that most fully and describe the Holy Spirit are "gift" and "love." Jesus gave his followers the gift of his own body and blood in the Eucharist. What greater gift could he give? Yet Jesus indicated that something wonderful was in store for them—a gift he could not give until he was glorified on the cross and had departed from this world. He seemed to speak with excitement and enthusiasm about this gift, even implying that it would be better than his own physical presence: "It is to your advantage that I go away" (John 16:7). St. Peter recognized this quality of the Spirit, for at Pentecost, he promised that those who believed in Jesus would receive "the gift of the Holy Spirit" (Acts 2:38).

Oil is another biblical image that symbolizes the Holy Spirit and his work. The prophets of the Old Testament used oil to anoint kings, to set them apart and strengthen them for leadership. Today, the church uses oil to anoint Christians in baptism, confirmation, and other sacraments. In each case, the anointing with oil represents and brings about the blessing and strengthening of the Holy Spirit. It is Jesus, the Messiah or the Christ, "the anointed one," who confers the Holy Spirit on those who are anointed. The *seal* of the Spirit is a similar symbol of being set apart and blessed by the gift of the Holy Spirit (see John 6:27; 2 Corinthians 1:22; Ephesians 1:13, 4:30).

The *laying on of hands* is also a symbol of the Holy Spirit's being conferred. Jesus blessed many people in this way (see Mark 6:5; 8:23; 10:16), and on a number of instances, the apostles also conferred the Holy Spirit by the laying on of hands (see Acts 8:17-19; 13:3; 19:6).

The Holy Spirit as a Person

Breath, wind, water, dove, fire, cloud, gift, oil, and *the gesture of imposing hands over a person*—reviewing this catalogue of biblical images, it is easy to understand why Christians find it hard to have a personal relationship with the Holy Spirit, why they tend to view the Spirit as a mysterious force or power. It is difficult to have a personal relationship with wind or fire! But as the *Catechism of the Catholic Church* (hereafter, the *Catechism*) indicates, these are only symbols of the Holy Spirit, not the Holy Spirit himself (see

694–701). They represent important aspects of the Spirit's identity and work, expressing attributes of a person who does not have a human face.

But Scripture presents us with some other titles and images of the Holy Spirit that introduce us to the Holy Spirit as a *person*. This is fortunate, because the Holy Spirit *is* a person, just as the Father and Son are persons.

In his Last Supper discourse in the Gospel of John, Jesus describes the Holy Spirit in terms that are uniquely personal. Because of Jesus' humanity, the apostles had come to know him in a very personal way as their teacher and friend. But when Jesus talked about leaving them to return to the Father, the apostles feared that someday they would be left alone, abandoned, or "orphaned" by God (see John 14:18). To reassure them, Jesus explained that he would send *someone else* in his place: "I will pray the Father, and he will give you *another* Counselor, to be *with you* forever" (John 14:16, italics added). And when Jesus observed that sorrow had filled the apostles' hearts, he insisted, "Nevertheless, I tell you the truth: it is to your advantage that I go away, for if I do not go away, the Counselor will not come to you; but if I go, I will send *him* to you" (John 16:6-7, emphasis mine).

Jesus characterized the Holy Spirit as a person when he referred to the Spirit with a personal pronoun—"him." Moreover, by describing the Holy Spirit as "another" like himself, to be "with" the apostles, Jesus implied that the apostles would have a relationship with this "new" counselor that was similar to the personal relationship they had with him. St. Luke, as well, treats the Holy Spirit as a person, when he explains that the Spirit can be "lied to" and "put to the test" (Acts 5:3, 9).

Who Is This Paraclete?

But who is this person that Jesus promised to send to the apostles in his place—this person whose coming would be so wonderful that Jesus would say, "It is to your advantage that I go away"? The Bible describes the Holy Spirit as an "actor"—that is, as a person who acts. Different English translations of John 14:16 use the terms "counselor" (RSV), "paraclete" (NJB), and "advocate" (NAB, NRSV, JB—from the Latin term for paraclete, *ad vocatus*) for the action of the Holy Spirit. The Greek word *parakletos*, translated as "counselor" in the Revised Standard Version, literally means "one who is called to one's side," and therefore "one who is at one's side." And, the Holy Spirit is clearly the person Jesus sent to be at the side of his followers after he left them. And yet, the Spirit is more than just a companion. In a footnote to John's gospel, the New American Bible explains further that

> the Greek term derives from legal terminology for an advocate or defense attorney, and can mean *spokesman, mediator, intercessor, comforter, consoler,* although no one of these terms encompasses the meaning in John. The Paraclete in John is a teacher, a witness to Jesus, and a prosecutor of the world. He represents the continued presence on earth of Jesus who has returned to the Father.[2]

The Counselor that Jesus prayed for is a *teacher* who will continue the instruction of the church begun by Jesus. "These things I have spoken to you while I am still with you. But the Counselor, the Holy Spirit, whom the Father will send in my name, he will teach you all things, and bring to your remembrance all that I have said to you" (John 14:25, 26; see also John 16:12-15).

The Holy Spirit is also a *witness to Jesus,* because he is the "Spirit of truth" who must testify to the full truth about Jesus. "But when the Counselor comes, whom I shall send to you from the Father, even the Spirit of truth, who proceeds from the Father, he will bear witness to me" (John 15:26). The first letter of John says that "the Spirit is the witness because the Spirit is the truth"; it also speaks of three witnesses to Jesus: "the Spirit, the water, and the blood; and these three agree" (1 John 5:7, 8). The Holy Spirit is the person who is on the witness stand before the world to testify to the whole truth about God. And as we shall see, everyone who possesses the Spirit also becomes a witness to Jesus. St. Paul declares that "no one speaking by the Spirit of God ever says, 'Jesus be cursed!' and no one can say 'Jesus is Lord' except by the Holy Spirit" (1 Corinthians 12:3).

John continues this legal metaphor or image of the Paraclete when he speaks of the Holy Spirit as the *prosecutor of the world:* "And when he [the Holy Spirit] comes, he will convince the world of sin and of righteousness and of judgment" (John 16:8). The Holy Spirit prosecutes or convicts the world of sin. But, at the same time, we might say that the Holy Spirit is the defense attorney for Christians when the world attempts to condemn them for their faith in Christ. (In fact, "defense attorney" is another good translation for the word "paraclete"; it is virtually synonymous with "advocate" and "counselor.") Jesus alluded to this action of the Holy Spirit as the Christian's advocate:

> When they bring you before the synagogues and the rulers and the authorities, do not be anxious how or what you are to answer or what you are to say; for

the Holy Spirit will teach you in that very hour what you ought to say. (Luke 12:11-12)

The Acts of the Apostles illustrates the truth of Jesus' promise many times. It shows Peter, Stephen, Paul, and others boldly defending their faith in Jesus Christ before Jewish courts, Greek thinkers, and Roman governors and kings, through the work of the Holy Spirit (see Acts 2:14-33; 4:8-21; 5:27-32; 7:1-56).

In fact, the Acts of the Apostles portrays the Holy Spirit's activity to such an extent that some people say it might also rightly be called the "Acts of the Holy Spirit." Throughout this book of Scripture, the Spirit is busy speaking (see 10:19; 13:2; 21:11; 28:25), consoling (see 9:31), sending people forth (see 13:4), deciding (see 15:28), warning (see 20:23), prompting (see 21:4), and even "snatching" Philip from one place to another (see 8:39)! He prevents Paul and Timothy from preaching the message in the province of Asia: when they came to Mysia and tried to go into Bythnia, "the Spirit of Jesus did not allow them" (Acts 16:6-8).

In the Acts of the Apostles, just as elsewhere in the New Testament, the Holy Spirit is presented as a person who is in an active, personal relationship with the disciples of Jesus.

Christian tradition provides another point of departure for exploring the question, "Who is the Holy Spirit?" From it we learn that the Holy Spirit is a person of God, the third person of the blessed Trinity. In A.D. 325, the church articulated its belief in the Holy Spirit in the Nicene Creed. In A.D. 381, at the Council of Constantinople (a council whose authority is recognized by Catholic, Orthodox, many Protestant and other Christians), the bishops of the church expanded this creed.

This council provided a response to a controversy that had arisen in the church of the fourth century about whether the

Holy Spirit was fully God and really equal to the Father and the Son. In response to these questions, some great works on the Holy Spirit had been written in the Greek-speaking East by fathers of the church such as St. Basil the Great, St. Athanasius, St. Gregory of Nyssa, and St. Gregory of Nazianzus. The result was the Council of Constantinople's affirmation of the full divinity of the Holy Spirit; it added this section to the Nicene Creed, which Catholics and many Christians profess today:

> We believe in the Holy Spirit, the Lord, the giver of life, who proceeds from the Father and the Son. With the Father and the Son he is worshiped and glorified. He has spoken through the prophets.[3]

Clearly, the early church recognized the Holy Spirit as a person whom we may address as "Lord," and whom we worship and glorify along with the Father and the Son.

Relating to the Holy Spirit

Jesus' way of presenting the Holy Spirit made it evident that his followers were supposed to relate to the Spirit as a teacher, a counselor, a consoler—as someone who would help and guide them in their daily lives as Christians. In the Acts of the Apostles, we saw that Christ's followers were in a dialogue with the Spirit, who actively directed and assisted them in their missionary activity. They knew the Spirit as the gift of Jesus and the Father to help guide and strengthen them, and they knew how to call upon the Spirit for his assistance. May we hope for the same experience?

Jesus taught us to relate to the Father as "Abba." The apostles and disciples—Peter, Mary and Martha, the "beloved disciple," and all the others—learned to relate to Jesus with warmth and friendship, each in his or her own way. How shall we imagine the person of the Holy Spirit in order to relate to the Spirit with the same depth of love and intimacy that we can have in our relationship with Jesus and the Father?

Recall the meaning of the term "paraclete": one who is called to be at one's side, a companion, a friend. Then, remember that, in John's gospel, Jesus says that in some ways the Holy Spirit will be even closer to the apostles than he was—as a teacher, counselor, and witness within their hearts. On the basis of those characterizations, I would like to suggest a personal image of the Holy Spirit that embodies all that he is and does for us: the Holy Spirit is "the friend closest to our hearts."

Granted, this is not a biblical image, but it is found in the fathers of the church. St. Cyril of Jerusalem taught that "the Spirit comes with the tenderness of a true friend and protector to save, to heal, to teach, to counsel, to strengthen, to console."[4] The *Catechism* describes the Holy Spirit as "the interior Master of life according to Christ, a gentle guest and friend who inspires, guides, corrects and strengthens this life" (1697).

Our friend the Holy Spirit is close to our hearts in order to set them aflame with love for God and with zeal to witness to our faith. He is close to us to convince us of our sin and to cleanse and purify our hearts. He is a friend strengthening us with virtues and gifts for the good of others and the church.

But most of all, this image of the friend closest to our hearts reminds us that the Holy Spirit is someone with whom we can speak and relate in an intimate, personal way. This image does not force us to put a "face" on the Holy Spirit, for he is a friend who is *within* us. It would be impossible, as well as unnecessary, to attempt to picture what the Spirit of God looks like as the gentle guest of our souls. We can simply speak to the Holy Spirit as that divine person who dwells within us, who is God's love poured into our hearts (see Romans 5:5).

Just as we come to the Father and the Son in prayer, then, we can also pray to the Holy Spirit. The *Catechism* poses the question, "Since he [the Holy Spirit] teaches us to pray by recalling Christ, how could we not pray to the Spirit, too? That is why the church invites us to call upon the Holy Spirit every day, especially at the beginning and end of every important action" (2670).

Our conversations with the Holy Spirit need not be lengthy or involved. As well as expressing the beautiful formal prayers of the church to the Holy Spirit, we may simply use short "aspirations" such as "Come, Holy Spirit"; "Holy Spirit guide me, give me wisdom"; "Spirit of holiness, show me my sin; help me to make a good confession"; or "Holy Spirit, give me patience." And, in times of urgent need or temptation, a simple "Help" will do! Anyone who has ever struggled with the formulation of a prayer can surely appreciate the Holy Spirit, for as St. Paul taught,

> Likewise the Spirit helps us in our weakness; for we do not know how to pray as we ought, but the Spirit himself intercedes for us with sighs too deep for words. And he who searches the hearts of men knows what is the mind of the Spirit, because the Spirit intercedes for the saints according to the will of God. (Romans 8:26-27)

God dwells in the hearts of Christians, and so the Holy Spirit is there, praying with us and for us and in us.

As Jesus assured his followers, Christians have not been left alone, desolate, or orphaned. Called to the side of Jesus' followers, the Spirit has become our teacher, advocate, counselor, consoler, and friend. He is a sort of second

Emmanuel—"God with us"—but even more profoundly, God *within* us. As St. Paul put it, we actually become "temples of the Holy Spirit" where God resides and abides (see 1 Corinthians 3:16; 6:19).[5]

Every image, however, is limited. Christians would miserably domesticate the Holy Spirit if we *only* thought of him as the divine friend within us. We cannot think of Jesus only as our brother, without recalling that he is also the omnipotent Lord of the universe and the final just Judge of the living and the dead. So too we must keep in mind that the Holy Spirit is also the majestic power of God pictured as tongues of fire and clouds of glory. He is the "breath" by which the whole universe was created and is held in being, and by which the dead, dry bones of Israel were raised up into a mighty, living army of faith (see Ezekiel 37). He is as incalculable and as free as the wind (see John 3:8); and, while he blesses and strengthens, he also convicts the world of its sin (see 16:8).

Out of pure love, like Jesus, the Holy Spirit condescends to come to our side from his heavenly might and glory; yet this friend remains the omnipotent and utterly holy God whose majesty and power we cannot even begin to conceive. The miracle is, like the miracle of the incarnation of the Son of God, that this divine person is not distant and impersonal. He has been sent into the soul of each Christian to live and remain as in a temple, to be the friend closest to our hearts—a fountain of refreshment and strength within us, the living water flowing from us and welling up to eternal life.

CHAPTER TWO

The Importance of Pentecost

While recognizing that each Christian is called to a personal communion or relationship with the Holy Spirit, we cannot neglect the role of the Holy Spirit in God's great plan to form and to save a people for himself. Sacred Scripture reveals this plan: despite the original rebellion of the human race against God in the persons of Adam and Eve, God's love was so great that in his eternal wisdom he planned to reconcile us to himself through an incredible act of mercy and humility.

While remaining fully God, God the Son became a man, Jesus Christ, and took upon himself the consequences of the sin and rebellion of every person who ever lived or would live. The climax of Jesus' saving mission was his *exaltation* in his agonizing death and his glorious resurrection from the dead (through which sin was forgiven and death was conquered), and his *sending of the Holy Spirit,* through which the power of Jesus and the life of God were communicated to the community of his followers, the church.

The Spirit of Jesus Poured Out for All

According to the Gospel of John, when Jesus was glorified by being raised up on the cross, the Holy Spirit was poured out upon the church, and all Jesus' promises about the blessings to be given through the Spirit began to be fulfilled. The Holy Spirit is revealed in John's gospel as the first and the greatest fruit of Jesus' death and resurrection.

In the Acts of the Apostles, St. Luke accentuates Jesus' promise of the Holy Spirit, along with his encouragement to await the Spirit's coming with expectation:

> And while staying with them he charged them not to depart from Jerusalem, but to wait for the promise of the Father, which, he said, "you heard from me, for John baptized with water, but before many days you shall be baptized with the Holy Spirit." (Acts 1:4-5)

Presumably, the disciples of Jesus had already been baptized with John's baptism of repentance when they began to follow Jesus. But John the Baptist himself had foretold a baptism to come:

> I baptize you with water; but he who is mightier than I is coming, the thong of whose sandals I am not worthy to untie; he will baptize you with the Holy Spirit and with fire. (Luke 3:16)

After his resurrection, Jesus announced that John's promise was about to be fulfilled: "And behold, I send the promise of my Father upon you; but stay in the city, until you are clothed with power from on high" (Luke 24:49). These were Jesus' parting words to his followers before he was taken up to heaven. How great the apostles' anticipation must have been! This mysterious event of being baptized in (or with) the Holy Spirit—the promise of the Father to Jesus' followers—was to be a moment that would transform their lives. They would be "clothed with power from on high." "When will this happen?" they wanted to know. But when they asked Jesus that question immediately before his ascension, he only replied,

It is not for you to know times or seasons which the Father has fixed by his own authority. But you shall receive power when the Holy Spirit has come upon you; and you shall be my witnesses in Jerusalem and in all Judea and Samaria and to the end of the earth. (Acts 1:7-8)

Jesus offered a simple answer to all of his followers' curious and troubled inquiries about when his kingdom would come and what they would do and say after his departure. *Don't be concerned or anxious, but be ready to receive the Holy Spirit, whom the Father and I will send.* The future life of the church after Jesus' time on earth was in the hands of the Holy Spirit. The destiny of the church would depend entirely upon its reliance on the Holy Spirit's power and guidance. This is the importance of Pentecost!

Little wonder that the apostles immediately returned to Jerusalem from the mount of the ascension and "with one accord devoted themselves to prayer together with the women and Mary the mother of Jesus, and with his brethren" (Acts 1:14). This, as mentioned earlier (see Luke 24:49), was done at Jesus' direction; it is the original novena (nine days of prayer), and the only one officially prescribed by the church for all Christians, at the Lord's command. There, in the "upper room," the Spirit led Jesus' disciples to choose a successor to Judas, Matthias (see Acts 1:15-26). There on the Jewish feast of Weeks, or Pentecost, the Holy Spirit came upon them "like the rush of a mighty wind" (2:2). Having been raised up and exalted at the right hand of the Father in heaven, Christ now unleashed (or "poured out") the mighty power of the Spirit that he had promised (see 2:33). The Holy Spirit "appeared to them tongues as of fire distributed and resting on *each one* of them," and "they were all *filled* with the Holy Spirit and began to speak in other tongues, as the

Spirit gave them utterance" (2:3, 4, emphasis mine). Two aspects of this account deserve special notice.

All receive the Spirit. First, we see that the gift of the Holy Spirit is unrestricted: he is poured out on *all* Jesus' disciples. St. Luke takes pains to emphasize this fact: the tongues of fire rested on "each one of them" (Acts 2:3).

In the old covenant, the Holy Spirit had been sent to certain people to carry out some specific work or purpose of God. The inspiration of the prophets and authors of the biblical texts to proclaim or record God's word is a prime example. Rulers such as David were anointed by the Holy Spirit for leadership, and, at various times, many others were empowered or led by the Holy Spirit in their prayers and actions.

But Pentecost is different: in Jesus' new covenant, *all* receive the Holy Spirit. The Holy Spirit is no longer reserved for a few specially chosen individuals but is lavished upon every one of Jesus' followers, just as Moses expressed the wish that the Spirit would be poured out in abundance on all of God's people.

After Pentecost, the Holy Spirit would be poured out upon all who came to believe in Jesus. Peter quotes the prophecies of Joel that in the last days, God will pour out his Spirit upon "all flesh" (Acts 2:17) and that "whoever calls on the name of the Lord shall be saved" (2:21). When the people respond to Peter's speech, he urges them,

> Repent, and be baptized *every one of you* in the name of Jesus Christ for the forgiveness of your sins; and you shall receive the gift of the Holy Spirit. For the promise is to you and to your children and to all that are far off, *every one* whom the Lord our God calls to him. (Acts 2:38-39, emphasis mine)

The Holy Spirit whom Jesus promised to send was offered to *everyone*. The same theme is sounded in the announcement of Jesus' Great Commission in St. Matthew's gospel: "Go therefore and make disciples of *all nations,* baptizing them in the name of the Father, and of the Son and of the Holy Spirit" (Matthew 28:19, emphasis mine). All who respond to Jesus' call by faith, repentance, and baptism receive the gift of the Holy Spirit. Why? The Holy Spirit is essential to the identity of a Christian. As we shall see later, it is only through the Holy Spirit that a person fully receives a new status and identity as a son or daughter of God.

And here is another expression of this universal invitation: "All are called to belong to the new people of God," which is the body of Christ, the church.[1] As St. Paul taught, it is by the one Spirit given in baptism that a person becomes part of the one body of Christ, the church (see 1 Corinthians 12:13). And so, among the many reasons for the gift of the Holy Spirit, the primary one is this: so that each person might belong to God as his son or daughter and as a part of his people, the church.

The Spirit *fills* those who receive him. The word "fills" also reveals the uniqueness of Pentecost. To be filled with the Holy Spirit, or to say that the Spirit has been "poured out," implies that the Holy Spirit has been given by Christ in the new covenant with a new abundance, richer than ever before. As John's gospel states, "It is not by measure that [Jesus] gives the Spirit" (3:34). To be *filled* with the Spirit means that the Holy Spirit now dwells within, or makes his home within a person. That person is made new and becomes a "new creation" (2 Corinthians 5:17), a son or daughter of God by adoption—and thus an heir of God's kingdom (see Romans 8:16, 17, 23)—and a temple where the Spirit resides (see 1 Corinthians 6:19). This is the gift God offers to all people, beginning at Pentecost. This *indwelling* of the Spirit by which God makes his home within us (see John 14:23) is a presence that *fills* us with the abundant life that Jesus promised.

But, was it really the Holy Spirit that the apostles experienced? It is possible to mistake this abundant new life in the Spirit for something else. This is what happened to some people on the day of Pentecost. They saw the disciples, who "were all filled with the Holy Spirit and began to speak in other tongues, as the Spirit gave them utterance" (Acts 2:4). Some of these onlookers "were amazed and perplexed, saying to one another, 'What does this mean?' But others mockingly said, 'They are filled with new wine'" (2:12, 13).

Today, when outward signs of the Holy Spirit's presence are manifested, we find similar reactions. Some people are "amazed and perplexed" and honestly wonder what it means. Others, like the skeptics at the first Pentecost, try to offer a human explanation, rejecting the possibility that the agent now, as then, is God.

To all those who witnessed the Pentecost event, as well as to all those who have read his words in Scripture, Peter explained the event's true meaning. Speaking in faith and in the power of the Spirit, he simply said:

> These men are not drunk as you suppose, since it is only the third hour of the day; but this is what was spoken by the prophet Joel: "And in the last days it shall be, God declares, that I will pour out my Spirit upon all flesh." (Acts 2:15-17)

Peter announced the dawn of the final age, the "last days" of this world, marked by the sending of God's final (eschatological) gift to the world: the Holy Spirit. He is the gift given to lead human history to its final conclusion and ultimate fulfillment. In those days, as Joel's prophecy reminds us, "it shall be that whoever calls on the name of the Lord shall be saved" (Acts 2:21).

Out of the Womb, into the World

The speech of Peter's recorded in the second chapter of the Acts of the Apostles is the newborn church's first public proclamation of Jesus Christ and his salvation. Like a child who cries out for the first time at birth, the church bursts forth from the "womb" of the upper room. In the power of its new life in the Spirit, it cries out the good news of salvation in Jesus Christ. Pentecost has been called the "birthday of the church," and so it is. For on that day, the church that Jesus founded came forth from the womb of waiting and prayer and burst into the world.

For Jesus' followers, this leap from womb to world meant big changes. Membership in the church was no longer limited to those who had followed Jesus during his time on earth or to those who had witnessed and believed in his resurrection. Now the church reached out to all: "Whoever calls on the name of the Lord shall be saved" (Acts 2:21). As Peter explained in that first speech, "For the promise [of the Messiah, and of the Holy Spirit] is to you and to your children and to all that are far off, everyone whom the Lord our God calls to him" (2:39).

It is true that questions later arose about what restrictions should be imposed on gentiles (people who were not Jews) who wished to join the church. But the principle of the solution was clearly given at Pentecost: the church reaches out to include all people. This principle echoed the approach Jesus took in his public ministry: he healed, blessed, and accepted all who had genuine faith in him.

Peter's Pentecost sermon focused on the identity of Jesus:

"Let all the house of Israel therefore know assuredly that God has made him both Lord and Christ, this Jesus whom you crucified" (Acts 2:36). But Peter's sermon also alluded to the importance of the Holy Spirit. After all, how were those Jews who were listening to Peter to know the truth about Jesus "assuredly"? The explanation lies simply in the Pentecost event itself. Peter explains:

> This Jesus God raised up, and of that we all are witnesses. Being therefore exalted at the right hand of God and having received from the Father the promise of the Holy Spirit, he has poured out this which you see and hear. (Acts 2:32-33)

Thus, the first proof of Jesus' lordship and exaltation was the visible, audible event of Pentecost, when the Holy Spirit that Jesus had promised was poured out upon the church. These people had not witnessed the resurrection of Jesus, nor had they seen him appear after the resurrection, nor could they see him exalted at the right hand of God. But they did see the Holy Spirit manifested in the power and signs of the Pentecost event. As St. Paul said, "The kingdom of God does not consist in talk but in power" (1 Corinthians 4:20).

The Church's Experience of the Spirit

One thing the Pentecost event clearly reveals is that the reality and presence of the Holy Spirit can be "seen and heard" in history and in experience. This theme is repeated throughout the Acts of the Apostles, as well as in St. Paul's letters and elsewhere in the New Testament. When the Holy Spirit comes to a person or a group—particularly for the first time or in a new way—there is evidence of his presence. Consider this account of the "little Pentecost":

And when they had prayed, the place in which they were gathered together was shaken; and they were all filled with the Holy Spirit and spoke the word of God with boldness. (Acts 4:31)

At Samaria, Simon the Magician "saw that the Spirit was given through the laying on of the apostles' hands." He "offered them money, saying, 'Give me also this power, that anyone on whom I lay my hands may receive the Holy Spirit'" (Acts 8:18-19). Simon may have misunderstood that the Spirit was God's free gift entrusted to the church, but he saw quite clearly the power of the Spirit and desired it for his own twisted ends.

Saul, after his conversion, was "filled with the Holy Spirit, and immediately something like scales fell from his eyes and he regained his sight. Then he rose and was baptized" (Acts 9:17-18).

At the "gentile Pentecost," when Peter preached to Cornelius' household, "the Holy Spirit fell on all who heard the word. And the believers from among the circumcised who came with Peter were amazed, because the gift of the Holy Spirit had been poured out even on the gentiles. For they heard them speaking in tongues and extolling God" (Acts 10:44-46).

Likewise, when Paul baptized a group of twelve people at Ephesus and laid his hands upon them, "the Holy Spirit came on them and they spoke with tongues and prophesied" (Acts 19:6).

It is evident that in the New Testament, the reception of the Spirit is not something theoretical, nor is it purely a matter of faith. The church was meant to know the Holy Spirit through its experience of him:

- "You shall receive power when the Holy Spirit has come upon you, and you shall be my witnesses" (Acts 1:8).
- "The Holy Spirit will teach you in that very hour what you ought to say" (Luke 12:12).
- "But the Counselor, the Holy Spirit, whom the Father will send in my name, he will teach you all things and bring to remembrance all that I have said to you" (John 14:26).
- "When the Spirit of truth comes, he will guide you into all the truth . . . and he will declare to you the things that are to come" (John 16:13).
- "And I will pray the Father and he will give you another Counselor, to be with you forever, even the Spirit of truth, whom the world cannot receive, because it neither sees him nor knows him; you know him for he dwells with you, and will be in you" (John 14:16-17).

Jesus taught that the Holy Spirit would be *known* by his followers as a teacher, a counselor, and a source of power—on this the gospels agree.

Through their personal knowledge and experience of the Holy Spirit, the apostles and the early church were empowered and guided in their mission and ministry. For example, the Holy Spirit directed St. Paul where to go (and where not to go) to proclaim the gospel (see Acts 16:6-10) and revealed to him that he would be afflicted and imprisoned (see Acts 20, 22, 23). Little wonder that Paul spoke and wrote with such assurance about the working and gifts of the Holy Spirit: he was living it! In the lives of Paul and the apostles, the Holy Spirit's presence was as real as the physical presence of Jesus during his earthly life. Jesus sent the Holy Spirit for this very reason—to continue to encourage, to teach, and to guide them.

Interestingly, in our own time, the Pentecostal movement began with tremendous power, as some Christians decided to take seriously the teaching of sacred Scripture about the presence, power, and gifts of the Holy Spirit. As this happened, all the works of the Holy Spirit that some scholars had argued were either theological symbols or works of God reserved for the primitive church began to appear. They were a normal experience for both Pentecostal Christians and those in the neo-Pentecostal or charismatic movement. It seemed that Jesus was inviting, or perhaps challenging the modern-day church to take seriously what he taught his disciples about the Holy Spirit:

> And I tell you: Ask, and it will be given you; seek, and you will find; knock, and it will be opened to you. For everyone who asks receives, and he who seeks finds, and to him who knocks it will be opened. What father among you, if his son asks for a fish, will instead of a fish give him a serpent; or if he asks for an egg, will give him a scorpion? If you then, who are evil, know how to give good gifts to your children, how much more will the heavenly Father give the Holy Spirit to those who ask him! (Luke 11:9-13)

The Fruit of the Spirit in the Church

Further evidence of the Holy Spirit's presence in the primitive church was the *fruit* that was borne in the community of the church. Here are the immediate results of Pentecost, as recorded in the New Testament's first account of the life of the newborn church:

> All who believed were together and had all things in common; and they sold their possessions and goods

and distributed them to all as any had need. And day by day, attending the temple together and breaking bread in their homes, they partook of food with glad and generous hearts, praising God and having favor with all the people. And the Lord added to their number day by day those who were being saved. (Acts 2:44-47)

Some scholars hold that this is an idealized picture of the first local Christian church in Jerusalem. St. Luke, they claim, is inclined to paint a rosy picture of this community and so avoids mentioning its problems and struggles. But if this is true, why, then, does St. Luke report the challenges and struggles of the young church throughout the rest of his book? Peter and John are arrested and threatened (see Acts 4). Ananias and Sapphira, two members of the Jerusalem church, are struck dead by God (see Acts 5). A bitter dispute arises between the Greek and the Hebrew Jewish Christians in Jerusalem (see Acts 6). The deacon Stephen is stoned (see Acts 7). And the difficulties go on and on. Life in the first Christian church was not a holiday from reality and human weakness!

So, what do we make of the description of the church in the second chapter of Acts? I would argue that it is an accurate account, because it provides a reasonable explanation for the rapid growth and attractiveness of this small community of believers in Jesus that was shunned by most Jews and suspected by the Romans. How would a group with so many liabilities ever grow? Only if other people saw something powerful, attractive, and extraordinary in it. And, of course, this is exactly what they saw: the power of God in the wonders and signs of healings and miracles; the generosity and joy of its members; their dedication to prayer, fellowship, and the apostles' teaching. These characteristics, Luke implies, were not natural phenomena (most church communities don't look like this today, either). They were a result of Pentecost, a fruit of the outpouring of the Holy Spirit.

Another view of this description of the fruits of Pentecost in the early church is that it was accurate but temporary and isolated. Yes, the primitive church in Jerusalem was like that, but only for a brief time, a honeymoon phase that soon ended. This view fits with the Acts of the Apostles' later accounts of difficulties in the community.

According to this theory, the church was never intended to live for very long in a euphoric state marked by joy, generosity, miracles, and praise. There is some truth in this interpretation. Trials and difficulties will inevitably come to the church. Some members of the church will sin seriously, and the rest will struggle with sin and prejudices that weaken the church and its witness. Remember, Jesus said that he didn't come to call the perfect and "healthy" to repentance, but sinners (see Mark 2:17; Luke 5:31, 32).

Does this mean that the church must inevitably lose its joy, praise, charity, and power to work wonders in Jesus' name? Not at all! If anything, the Acts of the Apostles describes a resilient church that was able to overcome its trials, confusion, and failures through its faith and by the power of Jesus Christ and the Holy Spirit. The community was sobered by the deaths of Ananias and Sapphira, but it also learned from them. The disputes over food distribution (see Acts 6) and gentile circumcision (see Acts 15) caused the church to discuss these issues and seek the Holy Spirit's guidance, which it received in both cases. The stoning of Stephen, as with most martyrdoms, actually strengthened the church's faith, and the persecution that followed led to new missionary outreach (see Acts 8).

As the history of Christianity unfolded, the power of Pentecost and the resulting attractiveness of the church of Jesus Christ did not wither and die. Many of St. Paul's letters to the early churches attest to the continuing grace and power of the Spirit.

Read, for instance, Paul's joyful and encouraging letter to the Philippians, written from prison: "Yes and I shall rejoice for I know that through your prayers and the help of the Spirit of Jesus Christ this will turn out for my deliverance" (Philippians 1:19). To the Corinthians, he wrote of the gifts of the Spirit given them: "I give thanks to God always for you because of the grace of God which was given you in Christ Jesus, that in every way you were enriched with all speech and all knowledge . . . so that you are not lacking in any spiritual gift, as you await the coming of our Lord Jesus Christ" (1 Corinthians 1:4-5, 7). In Paul's first letter to the Thessalonians, he announced,

> We give thanks to God always for you all, constantly mentioning you in our prayers, remembering before our God and Father your work of faith and labor of love and steadfastness of hope in our Lord Jesus Christ. . . . You became imitators of us and of the Lord, for you received the word in much affliction, with joy inspired by the Holy Spirit; so that you became an example to all the believers in Macedonia and in Achaia. For not only has the word of the Lord sounded forth from you in Macedonia and Achaia, but your faith in God has gone forth everywhere, so that we need not say anything. (1 Thessalonians 1:2-8)

The Secret of the Church's Growth

As the church grew and spread, the secret of its attraction and power remained a mystery to many in the Roman Empire. Historian Henry Chadwick observes,

Even to a writer as early as the author of Acts (probably circa A.D. 80), the expansion of the church seemed an extraordinary chain of improbabilities. Nothing could have been less likely to succeed by any ordinary standard of expectation.[2]

Chadwick lists many of the reasons why Christianity spread. Interestingly, the list culminates with that deep Christian love known as charity:

The practical application of charity was probably the most potent single cause of Christian success. The pagan comment "See how these Christians love one another" (reported by Tertullian) was not irony. Christian charity expressed itself in care for the poor, for widows and orphans, in visits to brethren in prison or condemned to the living death of labor in the mines, and in social action in time of calamity like famine, earthquake, pestilence or war.[3]

Among the other works of charity that Chadwick singles out as most notable are burial of the dead, hospitality to travelers, and almsgiving.[4]

Now, what is the source of Christian charity of this sort? St. Paul identifies charity, *agape* love, as the greatest gift (see 1 Corinthians 13:13) and fruit (see Galatians 5:22) of the Holy Spirit. "God's love has been poured into our hearts through the Holy Spirit who has been given to us," he notes (Romans 5:5). Little wonder that by the Middle Ages, one of the most important names given to the Holy Spirit, based on his works, was "Love."

If we return for a moment to the description of the primitive church in Jerusalem, we notice that its attractiveness had to do with either power or love. The *power* of the Holy

Spirit caused wonders and signs to be worked in the name of Jesus. *Love* took the form of fervent prayer (expressing love for God) or the sharing of possessions, hospitality, fellowship, and mutual support (expressing love of neighbor).

Here, then, is the importance of Pentecost, summed up in two words: "power" and "love." Not merely human power or purely human love, but a power and love that have their origin in God and are released by the life, passion, death, and resurrection of Jesus Christ (see 1 John 4:10). They were manifested as the power and love of the Holy Spirit poured out upon or filling the followers of Jesus, beginning at Pentecost.

Pentecost was not just a "flash in the pan." It was no temporary phenomenon that launched the church, captivated its members for a few short weeks or years, and then departed. Jesus did not give the Holy Spirit to the church—and to each local church or parish—only for a time. The Spirit was not leased to the church; he is a permanent gift. Nor did Jesus give the fullness of the Holy Spirit to the church at Pentecost, and a weakened, watered-down portion of the Spirit to the later church.

Pentecost was the beginning, but the power, gift, fruits, and grace of the Holy Spirit are fully available to the church today—they are here for the asking. Pentecost is significant not just as an historical event. The Holy Spirit, first poured out at Pentecost, continues to shine forth in the church despite its struggles, sin, and weakness. All the more reason why the church needs the strength and guidance of the Spirit in every age, since every age is a time of struggle and conflict until the Lord returns!

One may correctly observe that the particular work and manifestation of the Holy Spirit may look somewhat different and take different forms at different times in the church's history and in our own lives. However, it is always appropriate and important to ask what real difference Pentecost makes to the church. Do God's people expect the Holy Spirit to empower, enliven, and guide them in every age and every situation? Do we wait with expectant faith, like the first disciples, for the Holy Spirit to come upon us? The bottom line is this: do we believe in the Holy Spirit not merely as a doctrine but as a living person whom the church and each one of us absolutely needs every day to live fully as Christians? If so, then Pentecost really matters, and our lives and the life of the church will be continually and beautifully transformed.

I have always been struck by the fact that a season of celebration follows each of the two other great feasts of the Christian Church, Christmas and Easter: the Christmas season and the Easter season. But the day after the third great feast of the church, Pentecost, we return to "ordinary time," and liturgically, to the green vestments and normal cycle of biblical readings from the "ordinary time" of the year.

Why isn't there a special season to celebrate Pentecost? The answer, I think, is that the church always lives in the season of Pentecost, which is the last great event of Christ's mission until he comes again in glory to bring human history to a close and to judge the living and the dead. This whole age, the age of the church, is the season of Pentecost. It is the era of human history in which God reigns and reveals himself through the Holy Spirit. And we, the church, are a "pentecostal people," a people who live by the power and love of the Holy Spirit who was first lavished upon us at Pentecost.

CHAPTER THREE

The Holy Spirit and Prayer

*Abbot Lot came to Abbot Joseph and said: Father,
according as I am able, I keep my little rule, and my
little fast, my prayer, meditation and contemplative
silence; and according as I am able I strive to cleanse
my heart of thoughts: now what more should I do?
The elder rose up in reply and stretched out his hands
to heaven, and his fingers became like ten lamps of
fire. He said: Why not be totally changed into fire?[1]*

This saying from the desert fathers, the Egyptian ascetics of the fourth century, gets to the heart of the ultimate goal of prayer: to be aflame with the love of God. Christian teaching on prayer includes the different forms of prayer—vocal, meditative, and contemplative (*Catechism* 2700–19)—and the different purposes of prayer—blessing and adoration, petition, intercession, thanksgiving, and praise (2626–43). But the *source* of prayer is the Holy Spirit, who alone sets us aflame with God's love, as he did with the first disciples of Jesus at Pentecost. The *Catechism* declares,

> "No one can say 'Jesus is Lord' except by the Holy Spirit" (1 Corinthians 12:3). Every time we begin to pray to Jesus it is the Holy Spirit who draws us on the way of prayer by his prevenient grace. (2670)

The Holy Spirit, whose anointing permeates our whole being, is the interior Master of Christian prayer. He is the artisan of the living tradition of prayer. To be sure, there are as many paths of prayer as there are persons who pray, but it is the same Spirit acting in all and with all. It is in the communion of the Holy Spirit that Christian prayer is prayer in the Church. (2672)

Obstacles to Prayer

There are serious obstacles to prayer in today's world. A fundamental obstacle in the western world is the crisis of faith. The Catholic bishops at the Second Vatican Council found it necessary to specifically address the problem of atheism, which in its modern forms has been advancing steadily since the so-called "Enlightenment" of the seventeenth and eighteenth centuries.

How is it possible to pray with all the distractions of the modern world, in a climate so conducive to life without God, or even opposed to him? Certainly those who wish to persevere in faith and prayer find themselves in the midst of a tremendous spiritual battle. The *Catechism* devotes an entire section to "The Battle of Prayer" (2725–26), which is inseparable from Christian life:

In the battle of prayer, we must face in ourselves and around us erroneous notions of prayer. Some people view prayer as a simple psychological activity, others as an effort of concentration to reach a mental void. Still others reduce prayer to ritual words and postures. Many Christians unconsciously regard prayer as an occupation that is incompatible with all the other things they have to do: they "don't have the time." Those who seek God by prayer are quickly discouraged because they do not know *that prayer comes also from the Holy Spirit and not from themselves alone.* (2726, emphasis mine)

Invited to Intimacy

Prayer is a gift of the Holy Spirit, who is the "interior Master of Christian prayer." The greatest teacher of prayer, who engaged most fully in the battle of prayer, is Jesus himself. His teaching and example are the norm for what it means to be a Christian.

At the same time, Jesus' relationship with God was unique. Of all persons who have ever lived, only Jesus was at once *fully human and fully God*—the second person of the blessed Trinity, the only-begotten, divine Son of God the Father.

Jesus' relationship with the Father (whom he called "Abba," meaning "Dad" or "dear Father") was so personal, warm, and intimate that it was a source of scandal to his fellow Jews, and a source of amazement or consternation to everyone else. John's gospel sums it up succinctly: "This is why the Jews sought all the more to kill him, because he not only broke the sabbath [by doing good works on it] but also called God his own Father, making himself equal with God" (John 5:18; see also John 10:31-38).

Even more amazing than Jesus' unique relationship with God was that Jesus invited his followers to share in it, to know and approach God intimately as a loving Father. When Jesus' followers asked him to teach them how to pray, he told them to say "our Father" and to ask him confidently for grace, forgiveness, protection, and deliverance from evil, and the necessities of life ("our daily bread"). After his resurrection, Jesus instructed Mary Magdalene to "go to my brethren and say to them, I am ascending to my Father and your Father, to my God and your God" (John 20:17). To be a Christian is to enter into the same relationship of loving intimacy with God that Jesus had, to *become* sons and daughters of God, sharing in Jesus' divine sonship.

The Holy Spirit in Jesus' Prayer and Ministry

What is the *source* of our relationship with God as our Father? It is the Holy Spirit! If we are to understand how the Holy Spirit brings us into a relationship with God as Father and enables us to pray, we must understand this action of the Spirit in the life of the prototype of all Christians—Jesus himself.

Jesus, as a human person, had a fully human soul like ours (but without sin). Within the soul of Jesus there was an indwelling Spirit who motivated and guided him—the Holy Spirit. The Holy Spirit is truly the Spirit of Christ, the Spirit who lived within Jesus.[2] The Holy Spirit joined Jesus in perfect unity to his heavenly Father and was the wellspring of Jesus' power for his mission and ministry.

Because he was fully God, Jesus possessed the Holy Spirit from the moment of his conception.[3] The Spirit's presence was manifested—made public—at Jesus' baptism by John in the Jordan at the beginning of Jesus' public ministry. The Spirit of God descended on Jesus like a dove and rested on him, and a voice from heaven announced, "This is my beloved Son" (Matthew 3:13-17; Mark 1:9-11; Luke 3:21-22). Matthew's gospel reports John the Baptist's prophecy: "He who is coming after me is mightier than I. . . . He will baptize you with the Holy Spirit and with fire" (Matthew 3:11).

Jesus carried out his ministry entirely in the power and under the guidance of the Holy Spirit. Immediately after Jesus' baptism in the Jordan, the Spirit led ("drove," says Mark) him into the wilderness, where he prayed and fasted for forty days and was tempted by the devil. The first act of Jesus' public ministry, and his first response to the leading of the Holy Spirit in his ministry, was to pray—confronting Satan and the evil spirits in the desert. This was the first of many occasions when Jesus took extended time away from the crowds and the demands of his ministry to pray (see Luke 5:16; 6:12; 9:28-29).

Jesus Teaches Us to Pray

How did Jesus pray? The hallmark of Jesus' prayer was its intimacy and directness. Jesus knew God as his loving, dear Father, whom he addressed straight from the heart.

At the end of one of Jesus' prayer times, one of his followers was emboldened to ask, "Lord teach us to pray, as John taught his disciples" (Luke 11:1). Here, Jesus responded in two ways. First, he taught his disciples *what* to pray: "When you pray say: 'Father, hallowed be thy name. Thy kingdom come'" (Luke 11:2). This prayer—sometimes called the Our Father or the Lord's Prayer—was intended to be a heartfelt, personal address to the Father, just as Jesus prayed it. Formal prayers are not meant to become rote or dull, repeated unthinkingly or recited in monotones, but prayed from the heart!

Often overlooked is what Jesus told the disciples next: *how* to pray. In Luke's gospel, immediately after he taught the apostles the Lord's Prayer, Jesus instructed them to be persistent in prayer and ask the Father boldly to meet their needs:

"What father among you, if his son asks for a fish, will instead of a fish give him a serpent, or if he asks for an egg, will give him a scorpion? If you then, who are evil, know how to give good gifts to your children, how much more will the heavenly Father give the Holy Spirit to those who ask him!" (Luke 11:11-13)

Notice what Jesus says about the Holy Spirit here. He implies that the Holy Spirit should be the object of our prayer and that he is the most desirable of all gifts, the gift that the Father is most eager to give us. Why? Because the Holy Spirit enables us to pray and brings us into the same relationship with God that Jesus had.

Jesus wanted his followers to pray as he did. He taught them a prayer that summarizes the essence of Christian prayer. But Jesus also prayed spontaneously under the anointing of the Holy Spirit—something that he promised his followers they, too, would be able to do, if only they asked for and received the great gift of the Spirit. We see Jesus praying this way when the seventy disciples he had sent out returned from their first mission of proclaiming the good news of the kingdom:

> In that same hour he rejoiced in the Holy Spirit and said, "I thank thee, Father, Lord of heaven and earth, that thou hast hidden these things from the wise and understanding and revealed them to babes; yea, Father, for such was your gracious will." (Luke 10:21)

Under the anointing of the Holy Spirit, Jesus rejoiced and burst out with a prayer of thanks to his Father. Earlier in Luke's gospel, Elizabeth did the same. Upon hearing Mary's greeting, she "was filled with the Holy Spirit, and she exclaimed with a loud cry, 'Blessed are you among women, and blessed is the fruit of your womb!'" (Luke 1:41-42). Elizabeth's "Hail, Mary" was the first spontaneous prayer of the New Testament inspired by the Holy Spirit! As for Mary herself, her Magnificat (see 1:46-55) was her great response of thanksgiving to God for his amazing work in her and in the entire history of Israel. As the *Catechism* says, "It is the thanksgiving of the whole People of God, and thus of the Church, which Mary in her canticle lifts up to the Father in the Holy Spirit while carrying within her the eternal Son" (722).

Indeed, Luke takes pains to emphasize that prayer and praise were invariably the initial response of those receiving an outpouring of the Holy Spirit. The Acts of the Apostles records just how much this reaction characterized the life of the early church, beginning with Pentecost:

- "And they . . . began to speak in other tongues, as the Spirit gave them utterance" (Acts 2:4).
- The apostles prayed and were filled with the Holy Spirit once again at the "little Pentecost" (see Acts 4:23-31).
- Stephen, "full of the Holy Spirit," prayed aloud spontaneously before his death and as he was being stoned (see Acts 7:55-60).
- As Peter was preaching to the gentiles of Cornelius' household, "the Holy Spirit fell on all who heard the word. And the believers from among the circumcised who came with Peter were amazed, because the gift of the Holy Spirit had been poured out even on the gentiles. For they heard them speaking in tongues and extolling God" (Acts 10:44-46).
- At Ephesus, when Paul laid his hands in prayer upon a small group, "the Holy Spirit came on them; and they spoke with tongues and prophesied" (Acts 19:6).

How important is it to worship God through the Holy Spirit? Here is what Jesus told the Samaritan woman at the well in John's gospel:

"But the hour is coming and now is, when the true worshipers will worship the Father in Spirit and truth, for such the Father seeks to worship him. God is spirit and those who worship him must worship in spirit and truth." (John 4:23-24)

For us, too, the hour now has come: Jesus has come, bearing the greatest gift of God, the Holy Spirit. All Jesus' followers can now pray and worship God in a way that is truly pleasing to him.

A New Relationship with God

One reason the true prayer of Christians is so pleasing to God is that it expresses our new relationship with him through the Holy Spirit. Prayer is conversing with God, and this conversation must spring from a relationship between God and us.

Many people presume that because God created every human person, he must be in a relationship with every person. However, this presumption neglects the reality of sin.

The fact is that we are not born and do not grow up "naturally" knowing God. Rather, by nature, we feel distant or estranged from God, questioning his existence and ever rebelling against his revealed natural and moral laws. This attests to the reality of a source of alienation from God at work in us, which Christians call sin. "Original" sin is the state of sinfulness into which every person is born as a result of the first human sin of Adam and Eve. "Mortal" sin is a person's free, deliberate, and informed choice of something that is seriously opposed to God's will; it breaks the relationship between God and that person.

The good news is that Jesus has freed us from the bonds of sin. By his passion, death, and resurrection he has opened the way for the human race to once again find a right relationship with God. The gift, or grace, of conversion—of turning back to God—has been lavished upon the human race through Jesus. The theme of conversion (in Greek, *metanoia*) is central to Christianity, because every person needs to be converted, or turned back to God.

Jesus' redemptive mission of conquering sin and restoring us to God's friendship is completed by the mission of the Holy Spirit. It is the Holy Spirit who brings about the new family relationship by which we become sons and daughters of God. Those who are baptized, "born of water and the Spirit" (John 3:5), enter into God's own special family. We literally become children of God, and thus God is no longer a distant, omnipotent ruler but actually becomes our beloved Father. Sharing in Jesus' own filial relationship with God the Father, Christians can truly call God our "Abba," our dear Father. St. Paul explains this relationship in his letters to the Galatians and the Romans:

> But when the time had fully come, God sent forth his Son, born of a woman born under the law, to redeem those who were under the law, so that we might receive adoption as sons. And because you are sons, God has sent the Spirit of his Son into our hearts crying "Abba! Father!" (Galatians 4:4-6)

> For all who are led by the Spirit of God are sons of God. For you did not receive the spirit of slavery to fall back into fear, but you have received the spirit of sonship. When we cry "Abba, Father!" it is the Spirit himself bearing witness with our spirit that we are children of God, and if children, then heirs, heirs of God and fellow-heirs with Christ, provided we suffer with him in order that we may also be glorified with him. (Romans 8:14-17)

Pope John Paul II commented on these passages in his apostolic letter *Tertio Millennio Inuente* (At the Beginning of the Third Millennium):

Man cries out to God just as Christ cried out to him, and thus he bears witness that he shares in Christ's sonship through the power of the Holy Spirit. The Holy Spirit, whom the Father has sent in the name of the Son, enables man to share in the inmost life of God. He also enables man *to be a son, in the likeness of Christ,* and an heir of all that belongs to the Son (cf. Galatians 4:7).[4]

The Holy Spirit "Deifies" Us

We see the powerful work of the Holy Spirit first in Jesus himself. It was through the Holy Spirit that the eternal Son of God was conceived in the womb of Mary and received a fully human nature. The Word of God was divine by nature, but through the Spirit he became human, a man, as well.

The Spirit's primary work in us is just the opposite. We are human by nature, and although the Spirit does work to purify and perfect our humanity (making us more truly and fully human), his primary work is, through Christ, to give us something new that we didn't have naturally: a share in God's own nature, in his divine life. One of the central teachings of the Eastern (Greek-speaking) fathers of the early church was that God has become human so that man can become divine. St. Augustine, a father of the church from the Latin tradition, said, "Of his own will he was born for us today, in time, so that he could lead us to the Father's eternity. God became man so that man might become God."[5] This is called the doctrine of the "deification" of man, or *theosis.*

Obviously, such a concept, if misinterpreted, could be a scandalous heresy. Human beings do not literally become God in the sense of becoming God's equals. How is this to be understood? Jesus' dialogue with Nicodemus explains how this deification—this sharing in God's life—comes about:

"Truly, truly, I say to you, unless one is born anew [or "born from above," or "born again"], he cannot see the kingdom of God." Nicodemus said to him, "How can a man be born when he is old? Can he enter a second time into his mother's womb and be born?" Jesus answered, "Truly, truly, I say to you, unless one is born of water and the Spirit, he cannot enter the kingdom of God. That which is born of flesh is flesh, that which is born of Spirit is spirit." (John 3:3-6)

This new birth that Jesus talks about refers specifically to baptism. Through this sacrament, the baptized receive a new life—"spiritual" life—as they are "born of the Spirit." Didymus of Alexandria describes our rebirth this way:

The Holy Spirit renews us in baptism through his godhead, which he shares with the Father and the Son. Finding us in a state of deformity, the Spirit restores our original beauty and fills us with his grace, leaving no room for anything unworthy of our love. The Spirit frees us from sin and death, and changes us from the earthly men we were, men of dust and ashes, into spiritual men, sharers in the divine glory, sons and heirs of God the Father who bear a likeness to the Son and are his co-heirs and brothers, destined to reign with him and to share his glory.[6]

This new life in Christ and his church is nourished by all the sacraments, especially by the spiritual food of the body and blood of Christ, the Eucharist. The Eucharist not only renews the new covenant with the Lord but it sets the hearts of believers aflame with the love of God, leading us to pray. As the "Constitution on the Sacred Liturgy" of Vatican II expresses so beautifully, "The renewal in the Eucharist of the covenant between the Lord and man draws the faithful into the compelling love of Christ and sets them afire."[7] Didymus of Alexandria adds at the conclusion of the treatise just quoted,

> Since we are only vessels of clay, we must first be cleansed in water and then hardened by spiritual fire—for God is a consuming fire. We need the Holy Spirit to perfect and renew us, for spiritual fire can cleanse us, and spiritual water can recast us as in a furnace and make us into new men.

Abiding in God

The first and fundamental action of sons and daughters of God is prayer inspired by the Holy Spirit. As St. Paul taught, "God's love has been poured into our hearts through the Holy Spirit who has been given to us" (Romans 5:5); that love is first expressed in praise of God, who has given us this priceless gift of love and divine adoption. As a result of our adoption we enter into the mystery of the Christian life as a life of abiding in God and making our home in him, and he in us.

Jesus illustrates this reality with the analogy of the vine and the branches: "As the branch cannot bear fruit by itself unless it abides in the vine, neither can you unless you abide in me" (John 15:4). The First Letter of John expands on this relationship and explains the role of the Holy Spirit:

> All who keep his commandments abide in him, and he in them. And by this we know that he abides in us, by the Spirit which he has given us. . . . By this we know that we abide in him and he in us, because he has given us of his own Spirit. And we have seen and

testify that the Father has sent his Son as the Savior of the world. (1 John 3:24; 4:13-14)

These verses imply that we don't have to wonder whether we are abiding in God, and he in us. If we keep God's commandments (this point is stressed in all the writings of John and his disciples), we know the superabundant love of God. We abide in God, and God abides in us by the Spirit who has been given us—the Spirit who is the very love of God poured into our hearts (see Romans 5:5).

In a healthy love-relationship between a parent and child, the child does not have to guess whether the father or mother loves him or her—although the child might sometimes fail to appreciate that love, especially when the parents are administering discipline! Best of fathers that he is, God doesn't want his children to wonder either.

Sacred Scripture tells us clearly that God, in making us his children through Jesus, wants us to know his love and to know that he lives in us and we live in him. God desires us to know that Jesus is the Lord, the Son of God, the Savior of the world. And he wants each person to be able to say that Jesus is his or her own personal Savior. And once we know all this, God desires us to love him in return and to pray to him with deep personal faith and trust. "In this is love, not that we loved God but that he loved us and sent his Son to be the expiation for our sins" (1 John 4:10).

The Spirit Prays within Us

Another way that Christians can know the reality of God, who is love dwelling within, is that the Holy Spirit actually prays within us and is the source of all authentic Christian prayer. As we have seen, the Holy Spirit is the basis of the Christian's new relationship with God. Through the Holy Spirit, we recognize that Jesus is Lord and that his Father is also our dear Father, and we are able to cry out to him in our hearts.

Many of the New Testament writings speak of the role of the Holy Spirit in Christian prayer. We have already mentioned Jesus' conversation with the Samaritan woman about true worship, "in Spirit and truth." Jesus demonstrated true worship, of course, by always praying to the Father with the guidance and anointing of the Holy Spirit (who was revealed as "resting" upon Jesus at his baptism). The Acts of the Apostles relates how the gift of the Spirit at Pentecost inspired believers to pray in power. Given our human limitations, the Holy Spirit is a gift we sorely need, as St. Paul acknowledges in his teaching on prayer:

> Likewise the Spirit helps us in our weakness, for we do not know how to pray as we ought, but the Spirit himself intercedes for us with sighs ["unutterable groanings"] too deep for words. And he who searches the hearts of men knows what is the mind of the Spirit, because the Spirit intercedes for the saints according to the will of God. (Romans 8:26-27)

Most of us have experienced dryness in prayer or struggled with how to pray or what to pray for in a particular situation: what a great consolation, then, to know that *the Holy Spirit prays within us!* This is a reminder of the fundamental truth that prayer is a gift from God and not a purely human activity. In *Crossing the Threshold of Hope,* Pope John Paul II explained,

> *In prayer, then, the true protagonist is God.* The protagonist is *Christ,* who constantly frees creation from slavery to corruption and leads it toward liberty, for

the glory of the children of God. The protagonist is the *Holy Spirit,* who "comes to the aid of our weakness." We begin to pray, believing that it is our own initiative that compels us to do so. Instead, we learn that it is always God's initiative within us, just as Saint Paul has written. . . . Man achieves the *fullness of prayer* not when he expresses himself, but *when he lets God be most fully present in prayer. The history of mystical prayer* in the East and West attests to this: Saint Francis, Saint Teresa of Avila, Saint John of the Cross, Saint Ignatius of Loyola, and, in the East, for example, Saint Serafim of Sarov and many others.[8]

When asked about his own prayer, John Paul replied, "How—and for whom, for what—does the Pope pray? You would have to ask the Holy Spirit! The Pope prays as the Holy Spirit permits him to pray."[9]

One need only to have observed Pope John Paul II in prayer to understand these statements. The pope often became so immersed in prayer that he groaned aloud in intercession for the heads of the church, the world, and all of creation, as the Holy Spirit led him to pray and prayed within him.

Although the Holy Spirit does not intrude upon our human will, it is essential that Christians learn to open themselves and yield to the Holy Spirit in prayer (to be "led by the Spirit of God") as the late Holy Father taught us. Otherwise, we risk approaching prayer as simply another human activity that is completely under our control, where we do not allow God any access or "say." But although it does call for some effort on our part, prayer must be responsive to the Spirit of God, an anointed activity. As the *Catechism* succinctly states, "Prayer is both a gift of grace and a determined response on our part" (2725).

Glossolalia: "Speaking in Tongues"

The Holy Spirit is the source of all prayer. The sacraments, vocal prayer, meditation, and contemplative prayer already have been mentioned in this chapter as prayer forms through which the Holy Spirit works. Most Christians are aware that it is the Holy Spirit who enlightens the mind and heart in meditation or contemplative prayer. But if we are to discuss how the Holy Spirit is working *today,* we must also include the biblical form of prayer that St. Paul refers to as *glossolalia,* or "speaking in tongues."

Yes, this gift is controversial; some Christians question whether speaking in tongues is authentic or even desirable. And yet, hundreds of thousands of Catholics pray in tongues today. As a Catholic, I know that the Catholic Church, to be truly "catholic" (meaning universal or all-embracing), wants to affirm and embrace *all* that is from God and is truly Christian. If *God* is blessing people with a particular gift of prayer in our time, Catholics believe that there should be *openness* to it, because we wish to embrace all truth and all that God is doing.

Catholics realize that St. Paul valued other spiritual gifts more than glossolalia, but he did take pains to explain this gift so that it could be used properly in worship. He taught that the gift of tongues is desirable: "Now I want you all to speak in tongues, but even more to prophesy" (1 Corinthians 14:5); "I thank God that I speak in tongues more than you all" (14:18); "Do not forbid speaking in tongues" (14:39); "Pray at all times in the Spirit, with all prayer and supplication" (Ephesians 6:18). Glossolalia is a clear example of St. Paul's allusion to the Holy Spirit's interceding with "sighs too deep for words," or "inexpressible groanings" (see Romans 8:26).

Glossolalia (if it is indeed the authentic "gift of tongues") is a striking illustration of a prayer gift that must have the Holy Spirit as its origin, and yet also requires human cooperation and effort. It beautifully illustrates that prayer is both a divine and a human activity, requiring God's action and our cooperation. It can be copied or falsified but not reproduced by human skill or effort.

The authentic gift of glossolalia or speaking in tongues is twofold. First, just as much as a genuine gift of healing or working miracles, it requires God's action. Second, glossolalia requires a gift of faith to be received and exercised. God does not force anyone to speak in tongues; he does not force anyone to engage in any particular form of prayer. The person praying must "step out in faith" and yield to the gift, making sounds to allow the language of prayer to come forth.

Admittedly, speaking in tongues requires faith and an unusual degree of humility (at least for us "sophisticated" people of the twenty-first century who often have difficulty becoming like little children to receive a simple gift). Also, many people reject it simply because they do not understand it or because they fail to realize how it could benefit them.

And yet, even something as simple and apparently unnecessary as speaking in tongues serves to show the power and goodness of God's gifts through the Holy Spirit. It truly is a gift for those of us who "do not know how to pray as we ought" (Romans 8:26). Many people have found the gift of tongues refreshing and freeing; in it, the intellect rests from the onerous burden of formulating words and ideas, while the human spirit is lifted and quickened by the breath of God's own Spirit. Glossolalia is particularly helpful when words cannot easily express certain interior states, such as the heights of joy in praising God for his goodness, or the depths of suffering or sorrow. Some have said that Pope John Paul II's intercessory prayer (described above) was a form of glossolalia, that he prayed in a heartfelt way that was beyond the power of his own words to express.

Thus, speaking in tongues illustrates what St. Paul teaches about all prayer: that it is an expression of the divine life within us, of the indwelling of the Holy Spirit that makes each Christian a living temple (see 1 Corinthians 6:19), created to glorify God. We often forget that the essence of prayer is not a rule or a ritual. It is a lifting of the heart through the Holy Spirit to God, who is our dear Father, and to Jesus, the saving Lord, who loves us unconditionally.

Some Catholics may be tempted to limit their prayer to formal prayers or to the Mass and decide that glossolalia is not for them. And if Pentecost had not happened, then glossolalia—along with mysticism, or contemplative prayer—might well be seen as unnecessary, extraordinary, or outmoded. But, in fact, Jesus completed his saving action by sending us the Holy Spirit at Pentecost, and the Holy Spirit is always ready both to do new things and to renew the old and forgotten things that we find in Scripture and in our tradition!

An entire book could be devoted to exploring all the authentic forms of prayer that exist within the church. Here, it is enough to say that the Holy Spirit is the author and source of all Christian prayer. Let us call out to him to teach us and to enable us to pray at all times (see 1 Thessalonians 5:17). Holy Spirit, help us to yield to you as you inspire and guide our prayer!

CHAPTER FOUR

The Spirit of Truth

I am the way, and the truth, and the life; no one comes to the Father, but by me.

—John 14:6

Jesus is the truth. His entire ministry was devoted to living and revealing the truth that would lead his hearers to the Father and to eternal life with him. Jesus revealed this truth through his whole life—his words and his deeds. Often, though, those who heard Jesus, even his closest disciples, did not understand his teaching or the meaning of his works. The four gospels emphasize this point, providing many examples of this slowness to understand. Before we consider the work of the Spirit of truth, let us look at the blindness that characterized Jesus' followers before the sending of the Holy Spirit.

The New Testament records Jesus' warning against the "leaven of the Pharisees and Herod." The disciples ask what this can mean, since they have just run out of bread (see Mark 8:14-21; they apparently had forgotten that Jesus recently fed thousands of people miraculously). Again, as they head to Jerusalem, Jesus tells the disciples that there he must suffer, die, and rise: "But they understood none of these things" (Luke 18:31-34). Worse yet, Luke's gospel reports that immediately after Jesus gives the apostles his own body and blood at the Last Supper, they fell into arguing about which of them is the greatest (see Luke 22:24-29). And there is more: Jesus' betrayal by Judas, Peter's denial that he even knows Jesus, and Thomas' doubts about whether Jesus has really risen from the dead and appeared to the other apostles. . . .

Are these the men Jesus commanded to teach all nations (see Matthew 28:19)? The same ones who were told, "He who hears you hears me, and he who rejects you rejects me" (Luke 10:16)? Are these the apostles who are the *foundation* of Jesus' church (see Ephesians 2:20), which is "the pillar and bulwark of the truth" (1 Timothy 3:15)? Based on their sorry track record during Jesus' life, why should anyone believe in the infallible truth of the teaching of these apostles or of the church that was founded upon them?

The answer lies in something that happened at Pentecost.

The Spirit Will Teach You

Jesus was fully aware of the apostles' fear, weakness, and inability to grasp the meaning of his words and deeds while he lived among them. He did explain to them the meaning of many of his parables and challenging statements. But even that was not enough. They needed courage and wisdom.

I imagine that if I had been Jesus at the Last Supper and realized how little my closest followers had really understood the message I had been teaching them, I would have made one last great effort to explain it all. I might have said something like, "I still have much to teach you, so please pay attention (get out your notebook and paper) and let's go over everything one more time!" Jesus had a different approach, as we see from the account in John's gospel of Jesus' great discourse at the Last Supper:

> These things I have spoken to you, while I am still with you. But the Counselor, the Holy Spirit, whom the Father will send in my name, he will teach you all things, and bring to your remembrance all that I have said to you. (John 14:25-26)

This "Spirit of truth" would go on to explain even more to the apostles than Jesus had already taught them:

> I have yet many things to say to you, but you cannot bear them now. When the Spirit of truth comes, he will guide you into all the truth; for he will not speak on his own authority, but whatever he hears he will speak, and he will declare to you the things that are to come. He will glorify me, for he will take what is mine and declare it to you. All that the Father has is mine; therefore I said that he will take what is mine and declare it to you. (John 16:12-15)

Jesus was confident about entrusting the responsibility of teaching in his name to the apostles (and those who succeeded them) because he knew that they would receive the Spirit of truth, the Holy Spirit, to give them boldness and wisdom. The Holy Spirit would call to mind all that Jesus had taught them and also declare "the things that are to come."

The effects of the Holy Spirit's coming were evident at Pentecost. Peter, who had fearfully denied Christ, now boldly proclaimed the good news of Jesus with the clarity and power of the Spirit, who had just been poured into his heart. Similar accounts of the teachings and works of Peter, John, and the other apostles fill the pages of the Acts of the Apostles:

> Now when they saw the boldness of Peter and John and perceived that they were uneducated, common men, they wondered; and they recognized that they had been with Jesus. But seeing the man that had been healed standing beside them, they had nothing to say in opposition. (Acts 4:13-14)

In this transformation of Peter and John, Jesus' prediction was fulfilled: "He who believes in me will do the works that I do; and greater works than these will he do because I go to the Father" (John 14:12). The New Testament epistles that bear the names of these two apostles also attest to the wisdom that the Holy Spirit gave them.

But Peter and John were not the only ones who manifested the grace of the Holy Spirit in their teaching. When the deacon Stephen, "full of grace and power, did great wonders and signs among the people," the Jewish leaders disputed with him. "But they could not withstand the wisdom and the Spirit with which he spoke" (Acts 6:8-10). The whole seventh chapter of Acts records Stephen's teaching, culminating in his martyrdom:

Now when they heard these things they were enraged and they ground their teeth against him. But he, full of the Holy Spirit, gazed into heaven and saw the glory of God, and Jesus standing at the right hand of God. (Acts 7:54-55)

Stephen was stoned immediately after announcing this vision, with a young man named Saul consenting to his death. But Saul, too, came to know the power of God. This great persecutor of the young Christian church was miraculously converted by a blinding vision of Jesus, after which he was healed of his blindness, "filled with the Holy Spirit," and baptized (see Acts 9:1-19). A few days later, Saul (who came to be known as Paul) was found in the synagogue proclaiming Jesus as the Son of God.

Paul defended his discipleship on the grounds that he received the gospel through a revelation that came directly from Jesus (see Galatians 1:1, 12). But Paul also knew that his authority, however much it was guided and inspired by the Holy Spirit, rested upon his agreement with the teaching of the other apostles, especially Peter. Paul reports that in his first visit to Jerusalem, he spent fifteen days with Peter (see 1:18). Fourteen years later, he returned to Jerusalem to speak with the leaders of the church: "I laid before them (but privately before those who were of repute) the gospel which I preach among the gentiles, lest somehow I should be running or had run in vain" (Galatians 2:2). As a result of that meeting, the teachers of the church in Jerusalem confirmed Paul in his teaching and ministry. As Paul reported it to the Galatians, James, Peter, and John "gave to me and Barnabas the right hand of fellowship, that we should go to the Gentiles and they to the circumcised; only they would have us remember the poor, which very thing I was eager to do" (Galatians 2:9, 10).

Lessons from Scripture

From these accounts, we learn, first, that apostolic authority to teach and preach the gospel of Christ is a gift from God—one of the many gifts of the Holy Spirit to the church. Second, this authority to teach the gospel is tested and confirmed within the unity or communion of the church's apostolic leaders. Even St. Paul knew that his teaching, initially received by revelation from Christ himself, needed to be tested and confirmed by the other apostles, and especially by Peter.

Peter was not exempt from receiving fraternal advice and even correction from other apostles. After Paul recounts how he had submitted his teaching to Peter and the other "pillars" of the church in Jerusalem, he tells of how he was compelled to confront Peter with a lapse in his conduct. This was due to Peter's fear of the Jewish Christians who maintained the necessity of circumcision and who looked upon the uncircumcised gentile Christians as inferior. Paul bluntly told Peter that it was insincere and inconsistent of him to dissociate himself from the gentile Christians of Antioch whenever members of the circumcision party visited there (see Galatians 2:11-16). Paul does not relate the outcome of this confrontation, but the result is apparent in the account of the Council of Jerusalem (see Acts 15). There, Peter was a solid spokesman for full acceptance of gentile Christians, without requiring circumcision (see 15:7-11); influenced by Peter's speech, the council decided that men wishing to become Christians would not have to be circumcised.

What can we learn from the ways in which the Holy Spirit teaches the truth and preserves the church in truth? First, we understand that the apostles, as well as the elders who succeeded them, had a special gift and responsibility for teaching the truth and preserving the church by passing on the truth to future generations. Jesus specially instructed his closest followers, the apostles, in the mysteries of his teaching. He enlightened and empowered them at Pentecost to proclaim this saving truth to the world. As the Acts of the Apostles attests, the apostles did this, with the wisdom and power of the Holy Spirit to guide them.

Successors of the apostles proclaim the gospel. The New Testament epistles to Timothy and Titus describe how St. Paul entrusted the teaching office to these two men in the power of the Holy Spirit. Timothy was selected for this leadership by prophecy and then was empowered for it by the "laying on of hands," a prayer calling down the Holy Spirit upon a person for a particular ministry or blessing. The author of this letter (probably St. Paul) writes,

> Command and teach these things. Let no one despise your youth, but set the believers an example in speech

and conduct, in love, in faith, in purity. Till I come,
attend to the public reading of scripture, to preaching
and to teaching. Do not neglect the gift you have, which
was given you by prophetic utterance when the elders
laid their hands upon you. . . . Take heed to yourself
and to your teaching. (1 Timothy 4:11-14, 16)

Hence I remind you to rekindle the gift of God that
is within you through the laying on of my hands; for
God did not give us a spirit of timidity but a spirit of
power and love and self-control. Do not be ashamed
then of testifying to our Lord, nor of me his prisoner,
but take your share of suffering for the gospel in the
power of God. (2 Timothy 1:6-8)

Timothy is exhorted to boldly and consistently proclaim
the truth of the gospel. He has been commissioned for this
task through the laying on of hands, which is a primary
biblical precedent for the Sacrament of Holy Orders. Like
teachers of the truth in every age, Timothy would need courage and the ability to accept the suffering that comes from
others' indifference and opposition to the truth of Christ.
But as Paul reminded Timothy,

For this gospel I was appointed a preacher and apostle and teacher, and therefore I suffer as I do. But I
am not ashamed, for I know whom I have believed,
and I am sure that he is able to guard until that Day
what has been entrusted to me. Follow the pattern
of the sound words which you have heard from me,
in the faith and love which are in Christ Jesus; guard
the truth that has been entrusted to you by the Holy
Spirit who dwells within us. (2 Timothy 1:11-14)

The fullness of the truth that leads to salvation has been entrusted to the church, and particularly to its leaders, by the Holy Spirit. Defending the truth demands courage and will entail suffering. The author of these letters to Timothy foresees a time in which there will be debate and considerable confusion about truth. He is preparing his hearers for the situation he prophesies here: "The Spirit expressly says that in later times some will depart from the faith by giving heed to deceitful spirits and doctrines of demons" (1 Timothy 4:1).

Timothy is urged to constancy in these difficult times:

> Preach the word, be urgent in season and out of season, convince, rebuke, and exhort, be unfailing in patience and in teaching. For the time is coming when people will not endure sound teaching but having itching ears they will accumulate for themselves teachers to suit their own likings, and will turn away from listening to the truth and wander into myths. As for you, always be steady, endure suffering, do the work of an evangelist, fulfill your ministry. (2 Timothy 4:2-5)

These prophecies do not necessarily refer only to the "end time" immediately preceding Christ's second coming. They also refer to times like our own—to all those times when false teachings undermine the faith, and people depart from sound doctrine (which is always demanding and challenging) and turn to teachers who suit them.

The Holy Spirit unfolds God's truth. The scriptural solution to this crisis of faith is fidelity to the truth that has been entrusted to the church, and especially to its leaders, by the Holy Spirit. Jesus Christ himself was the greatest prophet or teacher to announce the fullness of truth through the Holy

Spirit. He promised to send that same Spirit to his apostles to teach them the truth! The Holy Spirit would gradually reveal the mystery of God and his plan. Christian truth, then, is not something purely static or unchanging, but it unfolds as the Holy Spirit enlightens the faithful who prayerfully reflect on and ponder God's revelation. This unfolding of Christian truth through the guidance of the Holy Spirit is beautifully expressed in a writing of St. Vincent of Lerins, a French monk of the fifth century:

> Is there to be no development of religion in the church of Christ? Certainly, there is to be development and on the largest scale. . . .
>
> The religion of souls should follow the law of development of bodies. Though bodies develop and unfold their component parts with the passing of the years, they always remain what they were. There is a great difference between the flower of childhood and the maturity of age, but those who become old are the very same people who were once young. Though the condition and appearance of one and the same individual may change, it is one and the same nature, one and the same person.[1]

St. Vincent goes on to compare the development of doctrine with the growth of a child into an adult, noting that "there is nothing new in old age that was not already latent in childhood." Catholics believe that all the doctrines that the church has defined over the course of centuries are latent in the teaching of Jesus and of the Holy Spirit in the apostolic age. The seed of Christian doctrine was planted then. Much of it was expressed in the inspired writings of the early church, the sacred Scriptures. The rest of the heritage of Jesus to his people was embodied in the way of life of the early Christians (practices, worship, moral teaching) that was guided by the Holy Spirit.

But how are we to distinguish true doctrine from falsehood and error? As St. Vincent said, "In ancient times our ancestors saved the good seed in the harvest field of the church. It would be very wrong and unfitting if we, their descendants, were to reap, not the genuine wheat of truth but the intrusive growth of error."

Who is responsible for guiding and directing this authentic development of doctrine? After his ascension, Jesus was no longer physically present to do this. But he commissioned others to carry on his prophetic teaching office—first, the apostles, and then their successors, the bishops. The pastoral epistles comment that the bishop must be an "apt teacher" (1 Timothy 3:2) and "must hold firm to the sure word as taught, so that he may be able to give instruction in sound doctrine and also to confute those who contradict it" (Titus 1:9). As a reward or compensation for doing this, "Let the elders who rule well be considered worthy of double honor; especially those who labor in preaching and teaching" (1 Timothy 5:17). The reward for teaching the truth faithfully is not primarily monetary; what is especially due the worthy elder is the honor of the other members of the church.

We might ask ourselves whether, in the church today, we honor (and listen to) those leaders who steadfastly teach the truth and govern the church well, despite persistent opposition and criticism. They are primarily responsible for carrying on Christ's commission to his apostles to proclaim and guard his truth through the guidance of the Holy Spirit.

The Spirit of truth among Christ's faithful. Sacred Scripture testifies that the leaders of the church, especially the bishops, are particularly responsible for teaching the truth of Christ that has been entrusted to them by Jesus and the apostles.

They carry out this task through the anointing, guidance, and power of the Holy Spirit. But what about the rest of the church? Isn't the Holy Spirit, the Spirit of truth, given to all Christians to lead them into the truth? The answer, of course, is a resounding yes.

The Holy Spirit dwells within every Christian, beginning with his or her baptism. As that person matures humanly and spiritually, he or she receives a capacity to grasp the truths of faith. However, it is important to distinguish between the natural capacity of the mind to comprehend things and the gift of the Holy Spirit that enables a person to grasp the real meaning and implications of their faith and of other truths.

The prophet Isaiah describes particular gifts of the Holy Spirit that were special marks of the Messiah (see Isaiah 11). Catholics believe that as Jesus' "messianic people," we too receive a share of these gifts, especially through the Sacrament of Confirmation. At least three gifts—wisdom, knowledge, and understanding—imply insight into truths that the mind cannot grasp without the Spirit's help.

For example, you can be taught that God is a loving Father or that Jesus is the Lord of all things and the Savior of the world. You might hear that Jesus is truly present—body, blood, soul, and divinity—in the Eucharist. These truths can be memorized items of information with no great personal significance—on the same level as addresses, phone numbers, and social security numbers. Or, they can be life-changing truths that come alive when you become fully aware of what it means that God the Father is "Abba," and you come to know his boundless, unconditional love. Or when you see that Jesus is truly your own Savior who desires to establish his lordship over every area of your life, and that this loving rule means true freedom. Or when, through the Spirit of truth, you grasp the life-changing significance of the real presence of Jesus—in the Eucharist, the sacraments, and the Scriptures, in the ordained ministers who lead and teach in his name, and in each and every Christian. These are examples of what we might call prophetic insight into Christian truths and their meaning. It is a gift of the Holy Spirit, for the Spirit of truth enables these truths to come alive.

Understanding our faith. One might ask whether it is really necessary to have this prophetic insight into Christian teaching. Isn't it sufficient to accept the truths of basic Christian beliefs such as the creed and assent to them without any particular insight into or experience of these doctrines?

Such questions reveal a certain view about faith: that it is a gift of God enabling us to believe in what God has revealed and what the church teaches, without necessarily understanding or having any interior conviction of the truth of these teachings. "If God and the church say it, then I believe it." This, as we will see, is not faith in the full sense that we understand it, at least as Catholic Christians.

Faith without any personal conviction of the truths of the faith is a rather bland, if not deficient, form of Christianity. Although it is all too *common* to accept the basic teachings of Christianity without a lively conviction of their truth, it is not *normal*—that is, it is not what God really desires for his people. We should think that God desires the truths of the faith to be matters of deep personal conviction and knowledge, which is a work of the Holy Spirit. In short, God desires the truths we believe as Christians to come alive and assume real meaning for our lives through the Holy Spirit.

As teachers of the faith, theologians and religious educators must especially rely on the Spirit of truth to guide them. The Holy Spirit must help these teachers with two tasks: first, to be *faithful* to the authentic teaching of Jesus Christ that he has entrusted to his church (the concern for orthodoxy or correct belief); and second, to teach these truths in a *dynamic* way, a way that makes them meaningful and alive for others, inspiring them to love and serve God more fully.

This can only happen if the Holy Spirit first works in the hearts of Christian teachers and theologians, inspiring them to proclaim the authentic faith of the church with a power that comes from the Holy Spirit himself. At the Franciscan University of Steubenville, we use the term "dynamic orthodoxy" to describe this necessary work of the Holy Spirit in making our teaching of theology authentically Catholic and vibrantly alive and attractive, because it is saving, life-changing truth.

Cardinal Newman's contribution. Cardinal John Henry Newman, a leading nineteenth-century Catholic, made a major contribution to our understanding of how we say yes to truth revealed by the Holy Spirit. In his book *The Grammar of Assent,* Cardinal Newman distinguished between the "notional assent" that we give to ideas or abstract concepts, and the "real assent" that we give to truths that affect our lives. Persons may be led to assent ("notionally") to some of the doctrines or truths of Christianity through the process of logic and reasoning. But real assent usually involves the whole person in a choice or decision that affects his or her entire life. Newman wrote that the assent of faith or belief is not merely notional—the assent to truths as mere propositions or concepts. Faith is a "real assent" that is personal, that profoundly affects the way a person lives. Here is how Newman expressed the need for the truths of Christianity to come alive:

Reading, as we do, the Gospels from our youth up, we are in danger of becoming so familiar with them as to be dead to their force, and to view them as a mere history. The purpose, then, of meditation is to realize them; to make the facts which they relate stand out before our minds as objects, such as may be appropriated by a faith as living as the imagination which apprehends them.[2]

Cardinal Newman expressed a simple truth that we all recognize. It is our heartfelt beliefs that motivate our lives and behavior. Our religious beliefs should be hearfelt, and not just ideas that we hold in the abstract. Religious beliefs are personal—they cannot be generic.[3]

Also, Cardinal Newman recognized that a person's assent to Christianity or to particular truths or teachings of the church is not something that necessarily happens completely at one moment or in the course of one event. Rather, this sort of assent is a matter of growth, which may take time and occur gradually, or sometimes suddenly unfold. The Holy Spirit, as Jesus promised, will guide the church into all truth, but he does not give a timetable or promise that it will happen all at once or in the same way for every person.

In addition, Cardinal Newman recognized the essential role of the church in passing on the fullness of Christian truth to the believer. For Newman, the statement "I believe what the church proposes to be believed" is not a purely intellectual assent to propositions: it is a real assent to all that the church proposes to be true through the guidance of the Holy Spirit.[4] It is an expression of what the Second Vatican Council, and St. Paul (see Romans 1:5; 16:26) call the "obedience of faith," the faith by which one "freely commits his entire self to God . . . and willingly assents to the revelation given by him."[5] The Second Vatican Council accentuated the role of the Holy Spirit in this obedience of faith:

Before this faith can be exercised, man must have the interior helps of the Holy Spirit, who moves the heart and converts it to God, who opens the eyes of the mind and makes it easier to accept and believe the truth. The same Holy Spirit constantly perfects faith by his gifts, so that revelation may be more and more profoundly understood.[6]

This living and ever-deepening knowledge of the faith is *normal,* not unusual, and is based upon the power of the Holy Spirit. As St. Paul commented on his own experience of preaching to the people of Corinth,

And I was with you in weakness and in much fear and trembling; and my speech and my message were not in plausible words of wisdom, but in demonstration of the Spirit and power, that your faith might not rest in the wisdom of men but in the power of God. (1 Corinthians 2:3-5)

Thus, an important work of the Holy Spirit in our lives is the work of showing us the truth, the work of *revelation.* St. Paul comments,

But as it is written, "What no eye has seen, or ear heard, nor the heart of man conceived, what God has prepared for those who love him," God has revealed to us through the Spirit. (1 Corinthians 2:9-10)

This does not mean that God reveals all truth directly and personally to each Christian, apart from his body, the church. If this were so, Jesus would not have needed to instruct his apostles and to commission them to preach and teach in his name. Just as the apostles needed Jesus' guidance, we rely upon the guidance of the church.

Public and Private Revelation

Catholics have long understood the distinction between private revelation and public revelation. Private revelation is truth presented by God to an individual or group for their own benefit and possibly that of others. But private revelation is subordinate to and always in agreement with revelation given by God to the whole church, which is public revelation.

Public revelation is truth revealed by God that he desires the whole church to know for the sake of human salvation. This revelation finds its climax in Jesus Christ, who is "the way, the truth, and the life." Thus, the period of public revelation ended with the death of Jesus and his apostles, who received this truth through the Holy Spirit even after Jesus had ascended to God the Father.

The Holy Spirit also enables the church to understand the complete meaning and implications of this public revelation more deeply and fully over time. This sometimes results in the definition of doctrines by the church centuries after the lives of Christ and his apostles. The Catholic doctrines of the immaculate conception of Mary and her assumption into heaven were not defined until relatively recently (1854 and 1950, respectively). These doctrines are not considered new public revelations, though, but truths implied in the biblical revelation about Mary. The Holy Spirit brought these truths to light and eventually led the church to affirm them as a necessary part of the full Christian understanding of God's revelation of his truth and plan. Similarly, it took the church some centuries to define the full divinity of the Son of God (at the Council of Nicea in A.D. 325) and the Holy Spirit (at the Council of Constantinople in A.D. 351). Not until A.D. 451 (at the Council of Chalcedon), did it declare that Jesus possesses both a divine and a human nature, yet joined in one, single, undivided person. This growth in understanding the fullness of Christian truth is what St. Vincent of Lerins was speaking about in his instruction on the development of Christian doctrine.

However, there is an important difference between this deeper understanding and fuller definition of public revelation by the church and the fuller understanding of the truth given to an individual Christian. Both are works of the Holy Spirit. One leads and preserves the whole church in the truth, while the other gives insight and understanding about the church's faith to an individual Christian.

The church as a whole, guided by the successors of the apostles, cannot be mistaken or deceived if the Holy Spirit leads it to define something as true. This claim is based upon Jesus' promise to lead his followers into the fullness of truth through the Holy Spirit (see John 16:13). The same protection does not extend to individual Christians. They need the Holy Spirit to help them recognize the truth, but they might not infallibly discern what the Spirit is saying to them, or whether every insight is truly from the Holy Spirit.

The Gift of Discernment

One essential gift of the Spirit of truth to the church is discernment, the ability to accurately distinguish truth from falsehood, and to distinguish the "voice," or guidance, of true, godly spirits from lying, demonic spirits. Discernment is testing whether something—a spirit, a direction, or a "word"—is truly from God and of God. It is also a judgment or testing through prayer of what God is saying, as Christians seek to know and do his will. This is a work of the Holy

Spirit, the Spirit of truth, who reveals the source of things and who desires to guide God's people in the way of truth.

Discernment leads to God's truth in many ways. It may be a matter of discerning whether a prophetic word at a prayer meeting is true prophecy or whether a reported "locution" or message of Mary or another saint is likely to be authentic. Or it may be discernment of a person's vocation or of God's will in a particular decision. St. Teresa of Avila highlighted the vital role of *knowledge* in discernment when she recommended that her sisters seek spiritual direction from those who are learned, as well as holy. St. Teresa wrote,

> I beg every superior, for the love of the Lord, to allow a holy liberty here: let the bishop or provincial be approached for leave for the sisters to go from time to time beyond their ordinary confessors and talk about their souls with persons of learning, especially if the confessors, though good men, have no learning; for learning is a great help in giving light upon everything. It should be possible to find a number of people who combine both learning and spirituality, and the more favors the Lord grants you in prayer, the more needful is it that your good works and your prayers would have a sure foundation.[7]

Learning is important, because the learned person may be aware of whether something is in conformity with or in contradiction to the church's teaching; someone who is holy but without learning may not know this. Like the other gifts of the Holy Spirit, discernment often builds on natural gifts and on the fruit of our labor, such as study.

St. Paul gave some directives with regard to discernment of prophecy. In his earliest New Testament letters, he urged his hearers to hold to the traditions they had received from the apostles and to discern or test every prophecy. Probably the most frequently cited text about discernment in recent Catholic teaching is taken from Paul's First Letter to the Thessalonians: "Do not quench the Spirit, do not despise prophesying, but test everything; hold fast to what is good, abstain from every form of evil" (1 Thessalonians 5:19-22). Paul also urged the Christian community in Corinth to first welcome and then weigh or test prophecies (see 1 Corinthians 14:29-32). Although these texts refer especially to prophecies given at prayer gatherings, they may be applied to any messages people claim to have received from Jesus, from Mary, from the other saints, and so on.

St. Peter agrees with Paul in warning against the deceptions of evil spirits and false prophets. He writes,

> First of all you must understand this, that no prophecy of Scripture is a matter of one's own interpretation, because no prophecy ever came by the impulse of man, but men moved by the Holy Spirit spoke from God.
>
> But false prophets also arose among the people, just as there will be false teachers among you, who will secretly bring in destructive heresies, even denying the Master who bought them, bringing upon themselves swift destruction. And many will follow their licentiousness, and because of them the way of truth will be reviled. (2 Peter 1:20–2:2)

False prophets and distortions of the truth existed not just in the early days of Christianity; they exist in *every* age. How can Christians protect themselves against these evils? By discerning or testing the spirits and truths that are presented in God's name. What keeps us from knowing the truth? John's gospel says that one reason is simply our choice to follow and love the evil inclinations of our own hearts rather than the light of God's truth in Jesus Christ. Discernment is needed here. The First Letter of John also recommends this discernment earnestly and warmly:

> Beloved, do not believe every spirit, but test the spirits to see whether they are of God: for many false prophets have gone out into the world. By this you know the Spirit of God; every spirit which confesses that Jesus Christ has come in the flesh is of God, and every spirit which does not confess Jesus is not of God. . . . By this we know the spirit of truth and the spirit of error. (1 John 4:1-3, 6)

One might be tempted to look upon this last passage of Scripture as quaint and interesting but outmoded. Today people do not listen to spirits and prophets, you may say. But are there not many voices calling people of our day to follow all sorts of "false Gods"?

Whatever we may call these voices, the test that John recommends still works. God has sent his light and his truth into the world as a man, Jesus Christ. Any spirit, prophet, or other source that has insight into spiritual reality and denies the lordship and deity of Jesus Christ is not of God; any who recognizes and confesses that Jesus is the Son of God and that he has come in the flesh is true and from God. As St. Paul says in 1 Corinthians 12:3, "No one speaking by the Spirit of God ever says 'Jesus be cursed!' and no one can say 'Jesus is Lord' except by the Holy Spirit." Although there are places in the world where people have consciously rejected the gospel of Christ, there are also places where people are ready to listen to the message of Jesus Christ through the church; hence, they are open to the Spirit of truth and can be taught by God.

The Ultimate Confirmation

Finally, in John's epistles and gospel, we find that the ultimate confirmation of whether we possess the Spirit—and the full truth of God through the Spirit—is love. True and correct doctrine means nothing without love (see also 1 Corinthians 13).

> By this we shall know that we are of the truth. . . . Beloved, if our hearts do not condemn us, we have confidence before God; and we receive from him whatever we ask, because we keep his commandments and do what pleases him. And this is his commandment, that we should believe in the name of his Son Jesus Christ and love one another, just as he commanded us. . . .
>
> Beloved, let us love one another; for love is of God, for he who loves is born of God and knows God. He who does not love does not know God; for God is love. In this the love of God was made manifest among us, that God sent his only Son into the world, so that we might live through him. In this is love, not that we loved God but that he loved us and sent his Son to be the expiation for our sins. Beloved, if God so loved us, we also ought to love one another. No man has ever seen God; if we love one another, God abides in us and his love is perfected in us. (1 John 3:19-23; 4:7-12)

As St. Paul says, "Knowledge puffs up, but love builds up" (1 Corinthians 8:1). The presence of the Spirit, who leads the church into all truth, is confirmed by charity, the presence of the same Spirit who is "the love of God poured into our hearts." In the next chapter, we will discuss how the Holy Spirit is further manifested, revealed, and active in the moral life of Christians, which is the life of love.

CHAPTER FIVE

The Spirit of Holiness

The primary work of the Holy Spirit is to make us holy, as God is holy. In other words, the Holy Spirit instills in people the virtues and character of God. This chapter will explore the twofold action of the Holy Spirit to purify our hearts, making them like the heart of God—aflame with love.

The first action of the Holy Spirit is to show us our sin—how we have rebelled against God and his plan and have fallen short of his glory. It is the work of the Holy Spirit to "convince the world of sin and of righteousness and of judgment" (John 16:8).

However, we would be in a sad state if the Spirit of God only revealed our sinfulness and left us in that condition. St. Paul observed that this is all that the law could do under the old covenant. But two of the greatest prophets of the Old Testament, Jeremiah and Ezekiel, predicted that a time would come when God would write his law on human hearts (see Jeremiah 31:31-40), and that he would actually place in us a new heart and a new spirit (see Ezekiel 36:22-28) that would enable us to keep God's law in holiness.

Through this second action, the Holy Spirit becomes a source of power for moral living. The Spirit enables Christians to follow the radical teachings of Jesus, to overcome sin, and to live in a way truly pleasing to God.

The Law of the New Covenant

The new covenant that Jeremiah and Ezekiel foretold was sealed by the shedding of the blood of Jesus on Calvary—the "blood of the covenant, which is poured out for many for the forgiveness of sins" (Matthew 26:28). In the Gospel of John, Jesus insists that his Spirit would be given to his followers, but only after he had been "glorified" on the cross (see John 7:39). Jesus' "great discourse" in John 17 ends when Jesus "lifted up his eyes to heaven and said, 'Father, the hour has come; glorify thy son that the Son may glorify thee. . . . Glorify thou me in thy own presence with the glory which I had with thee before the world was made'" (17:1-5). Finally, when Jesus was lifted up on the cross, "he bowed his head and gave up his Spirit" (19:30), allowing that Spirit to be released in the world. And when he was pierced with the soldier's lance, "at once there came out blood and water" (19:34). This is the living water that will flow from the heart of every believer: "'Out of his heart shall flow rivers of living water.' Now this he said about the Spirit, which those who believed in him were to receive" (7:38-39).

Who is this Holy Spirit who was poured out at Jesus' death? He is the law of the new covenant that was inaugurated and sealed by the shedding of Jesus' blood. Just as Jesus' tragic and horrible death resulted in new birth for the human race and a new covenant between God and man, it also marked the beginning of the new law for God's people that Ezekiel and Jeremiah had foretold.

In the Acts of the Apostles, Luke observes that the Holy Spirit was sent on the Jewish feast that commemorates the giving of the law to Moses on Mount Sinai—the feast of Weeks, or Pentecost. This is no coincidence. The signs of the descent of the Spirit in Luke are very similar to the giving of the law to Moses in the book of Exodus. Instead of the mountain, the setting is the upper room where the chosen disciples are gathered. In Exodus, only Moses is allowed on the mountain to receive the law, but in Acts the gift is given to all, as the prophet Joel's words stress: "'And in the last days it shall be, God declares, that I will pour out my Spirit upon all flesh . . .'" (Acts 2:17). The signs of the giving of each "law" are remarkably similar: in Exodus, a storm and fire on the top of the mountain; in Acts, a "sound from heaven like the rush of a mighty wind" and "tongues as of fire, distributed and resting on each one of them in the upper room" (2:2-3). For Christians, Pentecost is the feast of the giving of the new law of the Holy Spirit.

It is not just the outward signs, however, that illustrate the giving of this new law. Pentecost is an evident fulfillment of God's promise, given through the prophet Ezekiel, to replace stony hearts with "hearts of flesh" through the giving of a "new spirit" that will enable his people to keep his law: "And I will put my spirit within you, and cause you to walk in my statutes and be careful to observe my ordinances" (Ezekiel 36:27). This is the sign and promise of the new covenant: "I will put my law within them, and I will write it upon their hearts; and I will be their God, and they shall be my people" (Jeremiah 31:33).

The new law of the Spirit will be a gift for all people with the promise of forgiveness of sins: "For they shall all know me, from the least of them to the greatest, says the Lord; for I will forgive their iniquity, and I will remember their sin no more" (Jeremiah 31:34).

Not surprising, the first gift that Jesus gave his apostles was the gift of forgiving sins. In the Gospel of John, Jesus returned to the twelve on Easter day and fulfilled his promise to send the Holy Spirit: "He breathed on them, and said to them, 'Receive the Holy Spirit. If you forgive the sins of any, they are forgiven; if you retain the sins of any, they are retained" (John 20:22-23).

The Holy Spirit Reveals Our Sin

The Holy Spirit convinces or convicts us of our sin and conquers it. Let us examine these two main works in more detail, beginning with the action of God to convict the human race of its sin. St. Paul commented on the law of God revealed to Israel, beginning with Moses on Mount Sinai. Paul understood that this law of God was holy, for it revealed both God's righteousness and human sin. However, he also realized that the law was, in a sense, *deadly* for the human race because it revealed human sin without giving the power to overcome it (see Romans 7:7-12). St. Paul explained that even with the good and holy law of God, under the old covenant the whole human race remained in the bondage of sin and was totally incapable of overcoming it (see Romans 7:14-24; Galatians 3:19-24; 4:3). Humanity, under the old law, was utterly captive to "the law of sin and death," according to St. Paul (Romans 8:2).

What would put an end to the human race's bondage to sin and death—its unbelief, rebellion, and rejection of God? Ironically, the end of humanity's bondage to sin came through the execution of Love himself, the crucifixion of the incarnate Son of God, Jesus Christ!

St. Peter pointed out the *result* of the death of Jesus in his first public proclamation of the gospel on the day of Pentecost:

Men of Israel, hear these words: Jesus of Nazareth, a man attested to you by God with mighty works and wonders and signs which God did through him in your midst, as you yourselves know—this Jesus, delivered up according to the definite plan and the foreknowledge of God, you crucified and killed by the hands of lawless men. But God raised him up, having loosed the pangs of death, because it was not possible for him to be held by it. . . .

This Jesus God raised up, and of that we all are witnesses. Being therefore exalted at the right hand of God, and having received from the Father the promise of the Holy Spirit, he has poured out this which you see and hear. . . .

Let all the house of Israel therefore know assuredly that God has made both Lord and Christ, this Jesus whom you crucified. (Acts 2:22-24, 32-33, 36)

At Pentecost, when those Jesus gathered in Jerusalem heard St. Peter's first anointed public proclamation of the gospel and realized what they had done in crucifying Jesus, they *believed* his word and "were cut to the heart, and said to Peter and the rest of the apostles, 'Brethren, what shall we do?'" (Acts 2:37). Peter's answer was, "*Repent,* and be baptized every one of you in the name of Jesus Christ for the forgiveness of your sins; and you shall *receive* the gift of the Holy Spirit" (Acts 2:38, emphasis mine).

The Pentecost event is the initial great fulfillment of one of Jesus' promises about the Holy Spirit that is recounted in the Gospel of John:

Nevertheless, I tell you the truth: it is to your advantage that I go away, for if I do not go away, the Counselor will not come to you; but if I go, I will send him to you. And when he comes, he will convince the world of sin and of righteousness and of judgment: of sin, because they do not believe in me; of righteousness, because I go to the Father, and you will see me no more; of judgment, because the ruler of this world is judged. (John 16:7-11)

At Pentecost, the Holy Spirit is sent to convince the people of their greatest sin: their unbelief or lack of faith in Jesus, which led to their rejecting him and putting him to death. Therefore, the first work of the Holy Spirit in the moral life is to show us our sin—to convince us that we have sinned against God.

The Holy Spirit enables us to see, as Peter's hearers did, the reality and the horror of that sin, so that we are cut to the heart, as they were, and cry out, "What shall we do?" The Holy Spirit reveals *unbelief* as the root of sin and shows our errors in thinking regarding righteousness and judgment. As we shall examine shortly, the Holy Spirit convinces each person of sin through the *conscience*, that amazing God-given interior faculty by which we recognize good and evil.

In a culture that asks, "Whatever happened to sin?"—a culture in which the reality of sin is largely denied—can it be doubted that we need a resurgence of the Holy Spirit to convince the world of its sin? But what are the reasons for this denial of sin? As John's gospel states, the root is unbelief. People don't believe in sin because they don't really believe that sin is first and foremost an offense against a personal and loving God. They are not sure that such a God exists (or are convinced that he doesn't), and so the whole idea of sin doesn't make too much sense. In fact, we act like we don't need the word "sin" at all! Mistake, wrongdoing, crime, abuse, and so on serve the purpose better—and all the more so because "sin" still bears that uncomfortable connotation of an offense against God, which he might ultimately purify in purgatory, or punish in hell.

Another approach is to replace the concept of sin with a therapeutic notion. In this view, sin can be dealt with solely through counseling or some other form of psychological or psychiatric treatment. These approaches, of course, are often helpful or perhaps necessary, but they fail to deal with sin itself; rather they treat its psychosocial causes or effects.

Only the Holy Spirit can correct our mistaken ideas about sin. In the new covenant, the Holy Spirit is the law of God written on the human heart. The Holy Spirit is also the "light of conscience," the light or power by which the conscience can see clearly how God's law applies to our own moral choices and decisions. Christians also need the Holy Spirit to reveal how we have failed to follow God's law and to awaken our consciences to recognize our offenses against God and neighbor. This is the first and necessary step of conversion—of turning or returning to God: to acknowledge our sin.

On a practical level, Christians can and should ask the Holy Spirit to show them their sin and to grant them true sorrow or contrition for these sins. Any "examination of conscience" (a good daily spiritual practice) should include a prayer to the Holy Spirit to show us how we have sinned. We need such self-knowledge in order to truly know who we are and where we stand in the sight of God. As St. Francis of Assisi said, "What a man is in the sight of God, so much he is and no more."

However, it has been rightly said that anyone who really knew the depth and extent of his or her sin and knew how horrible a thing sin is would be crushed. Fortunately, God in his infinite mercy does not reveal the depth of our sin, even when we ask him, but only reveals what we can profitably understand and deal with. And so we can have confidence when we ask the Holy Spirit to reveal our sin, because God reveals sins in order to forgive them. Scripture tells us that God takes delight not in the death of the sinner but in his repentance, and so he is always able and ready to forgive (see Ezekiel 33:11, 19).

God's intense desire to forgive is often mentioned in Scripture. In St. John's gospel, Jesus first breathes the Holy Spirit upon his apostles so that they might forgive sins (see John 20:21-23). At Pentecost, Peter instructs his guilty hearers to be baptized in the name of Jesus Christ "for the forgiveness of your sins" (Acts 2:37).

The Holy Spirit Conquers Sin

In addition to revealing our sinfulness to us, the Holy Spirit enables us to conquer or overcome the sin in our lives. Through Jesus' death on the cross, sin was conquered, and the power of the Holy Spirit, the Spirit of holiness, was released and given to all who are baptized into Christ.

It would be tragic, and not a little ironic, if all that the Holy Spirit could do was to show people their sin without giving them the power to overcome it. But the good news is that in conquering sin and Satan through his death on Calvary, Jesus gave to Christians the Spirit of holiness and sanctification that enables them to become like Christ and to live in the peace and power of God's kingdom, freed from the bondage of sin.

St. Paul described the new law of the Spirit at work. He rightly assumed that the sending of the Holy Spirit at Pentecost would make a real difference in the lives of all Jesus' followers—in their ability to obey God and to follow Jesus' new commandment of radical love. Writing to the church in Rome, he bemoaned the situation he had endured under the law—knowing what was right, but being utterly incapable of doing it: "Wretched man that I am! Who will deliver me from this body of death? Thanks be to God through Jesus Christ our Lord!" (Romans 7:24-25). But this dilemma was resolved through the death of Christ and the sending of the Spirit:

The law of the Spirit of life in Christ Jesus has set me free from the law of sin and death. For God has done what the law, weakened by the flesh, could not do: sending his own Son in the likeness of sinful flesh and for sin, he condemned sin in the flesh, in order that the just requirement of the law might be fulfilled in us, who walk not according to the flesh but according to the Spirit. (Romans 8:2-4)

In both his Letter to the Romans (8:14-17) and his Letter to the Galatians (see 4:4-7, 21-31), St. Paul insisted that the Christian is no longer a slave to sin, living merely under a law, but has received the "Spirit of adoption" by which he or she becomes a child of God. Through the Holy Spirit, the Christian also receives a gift or an inheritance of freedom from the law, from sin, and from the "flesh," human nature in bondage to its passion and desires. In a word, through Christ we come under a new law—the law of the Holy Spirit—which means true freedom and the power to overcome sin: "For freedom Christ has set us free; stand fast therefore, and do not submit again to a yoke of slavery" (Galatians 5:1).

Does this mean that the battle against sin is over? No, a continual choice and effort must be made to live as a child of God in true freedom. St. Paul calls this "life in" or "according to" the Spirit:

So then, brethren, we are debtors, not to the flesh, to live according to the flesh—for if you live according to the flesh you will die, but if by the Spirit you put to death the deeds of the body you will live. For all who are led by the Spirit of God are sons of God. (Romans 8:12-14)

Paul goes on to explain that Christians are children of God and "fellow heirs with Christ, provided we suffer with him in order that we may also be glorified with him" (Romans 8:17). Living according to the Spirit is not an easy task. The road to glory is the same road trodden by the one who was completely filled with the Holy Spirit from the beginning, Jesus himself. For Jesus, this was a road of struggle, temptation, and suffering, as it was also for his Spirit-filled mother, Mary.

And yet, this life of struggle against sin is different and better than it was before the coming of Christ and the sending of his Holy Spirit. Two gifts/characteristics have made the difference.

The first of those characteristics is *hope*. Christians, possessing the Holy Spirit, have hope and an assurance of victory and eternal life, if they continue to live in the Spirit. St. Paul reassured the Christians in Rome,

> But you are not in the flesh, you are in the Spirit, if the Spirit of God dwells in you. Any one who does not have the Spirit of Christ does not belong to him. But if Christ is in you, although your bodies are dead because of sin, your spirits are alive because of righteousness. If the Spirit of him who raised Jesus from the dead dwells in you, he who raised Christ Jesus from the dead will give life to your mortal bodies also through his Spirit who dwells in you. (Romans 8:9-11)

As long as we persevere in following Christ and do not lose hope, we can trust that the Holy Spirit dwelling within us will conquer sin and lead us to glory with Christ.

The second characteristic that now helps us in our struggle against sin is *power*. Under the old covenant, many had the desire to live in a way that was pleasing to God, but they lacked the full power or ability to do it. St. Paul acknowledges that we do have a *choice*, a daily and hourly decision about whether to live according to the power of the Holy Spirit or not. If we choose to yield to the Spirit, the power of God is there. And so, Paul exhorted the early Christians (and us) to do it!

> For you were called to freedom, brethren; only do not use your freedom as an opportunity for the flesh, but through love be servants of one another. (Galatians 5:13)

> For he who sows to his own flesh will from his flesh reap corruption; but he who sows to the Spirit will from the Spirit reap eternal life. And let us not grow weary in well-doing, for in due season we shall reap, if we do not lose heart. (Galatians 6:7-9)

With the Holy Spirit, we have the hope and the power to overcome sin and reign with Jesus. The choice is ours!

The Holy Spirit Sanctifies Us

Christians are sanctified—that is, made holy as God is holy—by the Holy Spirit. Through the Holy Spirit, the Christian is transformed into the image and likeness of the "new Adam," Jesus Christ. St. Paul explains beautifully the Spirit's work of sanctification, making us like Christ the Lord:

> Therefore, if anyone is in Christ, he is a new creation; the old has passed away, behold, the new has come. (2 Corinthians 5:17)

Now the Lord is the Spirit, and where the Spirit of the Lord is, there is freedom. And we all, with unveiled face, beholding the glory of the Lord, are being changed into his likeness from one degree of glory to another; for this comes from the Lord who is the Spirit. (2 Corinthians 3:17-18)

"Unveiled face" refers to Moses, whose face became so radiant when he conversed with God and received the law that it needed to be veiled. In the new covenant, Christians need no veil as they see God face-to-face in Jesus Christ. And they are actually transformed into his likeness through the Holy Spirit. This transformation—the process of sanctification—does not happen overnight. It is a *growth* in holiness, a *progressive* transformation. As St. Paul says, we are being changed into his likeness by degrees, "from one degree of glory to another."

This process involves breaking from sin—continual conversion. It requires a daily turning away from sin and turning toward God so that we can see his face and thus grow radiant and be transformed. St. Theophilus of Antioch wrote, "A person's soul should be clean, like a mirror reflecting light. If there is rust on the mirror his face cannot be seen in it. In the same way no one who has sin within him can see God."[1]

Actually, the analogy can be applied in two ways: sin obscures our vision of God, like partial or total blindness; and sin also prevents us from reflecting or showing forth the image of Christ in us, just as rust on a mirror prevents light from being reflected perfectly. In order for us to see God and for God to be seen in us, we need to break from sin. And who enables us to do this? St. Theophilus tells us:

But if you will you can be healed. Hand yourself over to the doctor, and he will open the eyes of your mind and heart. Who is to be the doctor? It is God, who heals and gives life through his Word and wisdom. . . . For "by his Word the heavens were established, and by his Spirit all their array."[2]

To break from sin, it is necessary to acknowledge that sin exists; then we can turn to the divine physician for healing and forgiveness. When God passed by Moses in a cloud of glory, the Lord cried out,

> The Lord, the Lord, a merciful and gracious God, slow to anger and rich in kindness and fidelity, continuing his kindness for a thousand generations, and forgiving wickedness and crime and sin; yet not declaring the guilty guiltless, but punishing children and grandchildren to the third and fourth generation for their fathers' wickedness! (Exodus 34:6-7, NAB)

God does not deal with sin by ignoring it or pretending it does not exist. He does not "declare the guilty guiltless." He either *forgives* wickedness and crime and sin for those who repent of it, or he punishes the sinner.[3]

The Good News of the Spirit's Work: The Fruit of the Spirit

The good news is that through the Holy Spirit, God forgives sins and grants the authority to forgive sins in his name to his church. God gives the power to overcome sin and live a new way of life, transforming people into the image of Christ: "If by the Spirit you put to death the deeds of the body you will live" (Romans 8:13). Pope John Paul II, in his encyclical letter *Dominum et Vivificantem* (Lord and Giver of Life), noted that the daily struggle between "the fruits of the spirit" and "the works of the flesh" consists in the choice each person must make between submitting to or resisting the action of Holy Spirit in their life:

> As the apostle writes: "*Now the works of the flesh* are plain: fornication, impurity, licentiousness . . . drunkenness, carousing and the like." . . . . But he also adds others: "Enmity, strife, jealousy, anger, selfishness, dissension, party spirit, envy" (Galatians 5:19-21). All of this constitutes the "works of the flesh."
>
> But with these works, which are undoubtedly evil, Paul contrasts "the fruit of the Spirit," such as "love, joy, peace, patience, kindness, goodness, faithfulness, gentleness, self-control" (Galatians 5:22f). From the context it is clear that . . . the apostle is concerned with the morally *good or bad works,* or better the permanent dispositions—virtues and vices—which are the *fruit of submission to* (in the first case) or of *resistance to* (in the second case) *the saving action of the Holy Spirit.*[4]

If a person yields to "the saving action of the Holy Spirit," that person receives the strength to overcome sin, and hence knows how to live in the freedom and peace of the children of God. The sign that a person is living according to the Holy Spirit and growing into the image of Christ is that the person will display increasingly the fruit of the Holy Spirit.

Just as the quality of a fruit tree is known by the fruit it produces, so the depth or quality of a Christian's life is known by the fruit it bears, the fruit of the Spirit. And, of course, the greatest fruit is *love.* The Christian who lives by the Spirit fulfills Jesus' new commandment to love each other as he has loved us.

What Is True Holiness?

Understanding the meaning of living by the Spirit has many practical implications in the Christian life. For one thing, it sheds light on what it means to be a "spiritual person" or a "holy person." It is common for some Catholics to consider spiritual or holy a person who spends a good deal of time in prayer or performs pious acts, such as visiting churches, having a devotion to certain saints, or carrying a rosary. Others might view a person as spiritual or holy who doesn't drink or use profanity. Although these characteristics may be related or lead to holiness, a surer measure of holiness might be whether a person consistently manifests the "fruit of the Spirit" and acts toward God and others, as Jesus did, in sacrificial love and service. Only God sees the human heart, and it is not our task to judge or measure the holiness of others. But if *we* are striving to be a holy or spiritual people ourselves, it helps to have some idea what genuine holiness looks like.

The Second Vatican Council taught that *all* Christ's faithful people "are called to holiness, that is 'to the fullness of Christian life and to the perfection of charity.'"[5] In his apostolic exhortation on the laity, *Christifideles Laici,* Pope John Paul II recalled this teaching and added that holiness is the greatest testimony of the dignity conferred on a disciple of Christ.[6]

The pursuit of holiness involves a continual "renewal of Christian life based on the gospel," John Paul II remarked in the same document. "It is ever more urgent that today all Christians take up again the way of the gospel renewal." The pope encouraged all Christians to welcome "the invitation expressed by the apostle Peter, 'to be holy in all your conduct' (1 Peter 1:15)," and to follow "the exhortation of the 1985 Extraordinary Synod of Bishops, who said: 'Men and women saints have always been the source and origin of renewal in the most difficult circumstances in the church's history. Today we have the greatest need of saints whom we must assiduously beg God to raise up.'"

But, again we must ask, what is the source of holiness and what does a holy person look like—that is, what makes him or her holy? The Holy Spirit is the source of holiness, as we see in Jesus himself. Again, according to *Christifideles Laici*, "The Spirit that sanctified the human nature of Jesus in Mary's virginal womb (cf. Luke 1:35) is the same Spirit that is abiding and working in the church to communicate to her the holiness of the Son of God made man."

What does this holiness look like? The late pope presented a wonderful summary:

Life according to the Spirit, whose fruit is holiness (cf. Romans 6:22; Galatians 5:22), stirs up every baptized person and requires each to *follow and imitate Jesus Christ* in embracing the Beatitudes: in listening and meditating on the word of God; in conscious and active participation in the liturgical and sacramental life of the Church; in personal prayer; in family or in community; in the hunger and thirst for justice; in the practice of the commandment of love in all circumstances of life and service to the brethren, especially the least, the poor and the suffering.

In short, holiness does not consist in pious practices, but in following Christ and in living the Beatitudes by the power of the Holy Spirit! In a nutshell, holiness looks like Jesus Christ.

The Sin Against the Holy Spirit

God is always ready to forgive the repentant sinner. However, there is one sin that the sacred Scripture calls "unforgivable" (Mark 3:28f). The one sin that Jesus claimed would not be forgiven was the "sin against the Holy Spirit" (see Matthew 12:31; Mark 3:29; Luke 12:10). What is this sin? And how can any sin be unforgivable?

Earlier we saw that Jesus sent the Holy Spirit to "convince the world concerning sin" (John 16:8). Pope John Paul II explained that this involves a double gift: "The Holy Spirit points out or reveals the sin and thus the need for conversion, *and* the Holy Spirit gives confidence of God's mercy and forgiveness to remove that sin through the redemptive work of Christ, carried out by the Holy Spirit." As the pope stated,

> Thus in this "convincing concerning sin" we discover *a double gift:* the gift of the truth of conscience and the gift of the certainty of redemption. The Spirit of truth is the Counselor.[7]

Sin against the Holy Spirit involves either a refusal to repent—that is, a refusal to acknowledge one's sins when the Holy Spirit points them out (the Bible calls this hardness of heart—see Psalm 81:13; Jeremiah 7:24; Mark 3:5) or a refusal to accept God's forgiveness, which Christ offers through the Holy Spirit. One cannot be forgiven if one rejects the agent through which forgiveness is extended. That is why the sin against the Holy Spirit is unforgivable—not because God is unwilling to forgive, but because the person refuses to accept God's forgiveness through the Holy Spirit. As Pope John Paul II explains, the sin of "blasphemy" against the Holy Spirit does not properly consist in offending against the Holy Spirit in words; it consists rather *in the refusal to accept the salvation which God offers to men through the Holy Spirit,* working through the power of the cross. . . . The blasphemy against the Holy Spirit consists precisely in *the radical refusal to accept this forgiveness,* of which he [the Holy Spirit] is the intimate giver and which presupposes the genuine conversion which he brings about in the conscience.[8]

All this bears directly upon the situation of much of the modern world, which refuses to acknowledge the *existence* of sin, much less the fact of its own multitudinous sins against God and humanity. Pope John Paul II explained that, in our own times, what sacred Scripture calls hardness of heart "is perhaps reflected in the *loss of the sense* of sin."[9]

What are we to do in such a situation? We can pray for a reawakening of human consciences, said the pope, "that their healthy sensitivity with regard to good and evil will not be blunted." This is the Spirit's work, as we have seen, and as the pope went on to say, "This integrity and sensitivity are profoundly linked to the intimate action of the Spirit of truth. In this light the exhortations of Saint Paul assume particular eloquence: 'Do not quench the Spirit'; 'Do not grieve the Holy Spirit' (1 Thessalonians 5:19; Ephesians 4:30)."

What we have most to fear in modern culture is that people's consciences are being so desensitized to sin by constant exposure to violence, sexual promiscuity, disrespect for human life and dignity, and so on, that we are quenching the light of the Holy Spirit in human consciences and choosing sin as our way of life. Pope John Paul II made this appeal to us all:

But above all the Church constantly implores with the greatest fervor *that there will be no increase* in the world of the sin that the gospel calls "blasphemy against the Holy Spirit." Rather, she prays that it will *decrease* in human souls—and consequently in the forms and structures of society itself—and that it will make room for that openness of conscience necessary for the saving action of the Holy Spirit. The Church prays that the dangerous sin against the Spirit will give way to a holy readiness to accept his mission as the Counselor, when he comes to "convince the world concerning sin, and righteousness and judgment."[10]

Let us then pray for the Holy Spirit of God to convince the world and each one of us of our sin and to forgive and free us from that sin. Let the Holy Spirit sow and nourish in us the good fruits that Christ has won for us by his victory upon the cross. May the Holy Spirit continue to make us holy, transforming us into the likeness of Christ from one degree of glory to another!

CHAPTER SIX

Evangelization: Where's the Power?

After almost two thousand years of Christianity, how are we doing in fulfilling Jesus' parting mandate to his followers: "Go therefore and make disciples of all nations" (Matthew 28:19)? Not so well, it seems. As the world's population continues to grow, the percentage of people who call themselves Christian is gradually shrinking.

A 1985 Vatican study estimated that 3.2 billion people—about two-thirds of the world's population—do not believe in Jesus Christ as their Lord and Savior. They do not yet know that God himself has come into the world to save the human race from the bondage of sin, and to bring hope, strength, and life—even an eternal life of joy with him. Only about one-fifth of the people in the world identify themselves as Catholics.

Jesus' words are still as relevant today as when he walked the earth: "The harvest is plentiful, but the laborers are few; pray therefore the Lord of the harvest to send out laborers into his harvest" (Luke 10:2). Where, then, are the laborers? Where are the Christians who are out making disciples of all people? All of us have been given this commission by Christ, but how many Catholics do you know who are filled with zeal to spread the good news of Jesus to others? There are so few that Pope John Paul II had to call for a "great effort" and prayer to "re-evangelize" the many places of the world (such as Europe and the Americas) that had been Christian for centuries but now appear to have lost their Christian or Catholic faith, or at least the desire and fervor to witness to that faith. We are reminded of Jesus' words, "You are the salt of the earth; but if salt has lost its taste, how shall its saltness be restored?" (Matthew 5:13).

Because of this situation, evangelization has become a frequently discussed topic in the Catholic Church. There are bishops, priests, religious, and lay people who have begun to speak out about the need to evangelize, and have become evangelizers themselves. We should praise God for their efforts, because the church that does not evangelize—does not actively witness its faith to others—is dying, or dead. Most Catholics, however, still look upon evangelization and witnessing with indifference, suspicion, or disdain—either as a strictly Protestant activity or as something that is done by religious and priests or by foreign missionaries, but not by "ordinary" laypeople. In fact, today sharing one's faith with others is generally frowned upon; it is seen as forcing one's personal (that is, private) opinions on others. So most Catholics "sit on their hands" when it comes to witnessing to their faith.

The Difference That Pentecost Made

The apostles and other disciples who had encountered Jesus risen from the dead didn't witness to their faith very much at first, either. They didn't immediately tell everyone about the resurrection. They either continued to meet privately in Jerusalem, or, according to another account, they went back to Galilee and fished.

The evangelist Luke recounts that Jesus had instructed his followers "not to depart from Jerusalem, but to wait for the promise of the Father, which, he said, 'you heard from me, for John baptized with water, but before many days you shall be baptized with the Holy Spirit'" (Acts 1:4-5). Jesus promised, "You shall receive power when the Holy Spirit has come upon you; and you shall be my witnesses in

Jerusalem and in all Judea and Samaria and to the end of the earth" (Acts 1:8). Obedient to Jesus' words, the apostles went back to the upper room where they were staying and "with one accord devoted themselves to prayer, together with the women and Mary the mother of Jesus, and with his brethren" (Acts 1:14).

Gathered in that place when the day of Pentecost came, "they were all filled with the Holy Spirit and began to speak with other tongues, as the Spirit gave them utterance" (Acts 2:4). Peter, who had denied even knowing Christ, burst forth from the upper room, boldly proclaiming the good news of Jesus' resurrection and explaining that Jesus' death atoned for the sins of all. Peter also explained, "Being therefore exalted at the right hand of God, and having received from the Father the promise of the Holy Spirit, he has poured out this [Holy Spirit] which you see and hear" (Acts 2:33).

What happened when Jesus sent the Holy Spirit to his followers at Pentecost? The church of Jesus Christ was born. It was sent out of the womb and into the world and was launched into its mission of bold witness to Jesus' lordship by the Holy Spirit's power. The Acts of the Apostles is an extended account of the result of Pentecost: the growth of the newborn church and its powerful witness to Christ through miracles, signs, and proclamation. Although the apostles were especially commissioned and sent by Christ to evangelize, every Christian was a witness in the early church.

It is significant that the first Christian who was martyred for witnessing to his faith in Christ was not an apostle, but a deacon, or "servant" in the church. Stephen had been chosen to distribute food—hardly a glamorous task—and yet he gave powerful testimony to his faith when he was on trial before the Jewish authorities. His witness cost him his life; indeed, the word "martyr" literally means "witness."

As Tertullian taught, the blood of martyrs is the seed of the church. St. Stephen's testimony certainly had something to do with Paul's conversion (see Acts 7:58–8:1; 9:1-22). The second half of the Acts of the Apostles recounts the heroic missionary exploits of this same Paul, who went from being a persecutor of Christians to being "the apostle" or the "apostle to the gentiles."

The Spontaneous Expansion of the Church

The mission of the church is a continuation and extension of the mission of Jesus. It is humbling to think that Jesus left the completion of his work—either for success or failure—in the hands of those who had come to believe in him. In a certain sense, the salvation of the world depended (and depends) on the work of Jesus' followers. Unless people hear the truth and the message of Jesus proclaimed to them, they cannot accept and believe in God's saving work.

> For, "everyone who calls upon the name of the Lord will be saved." But how are men to call upon him in whom they have not believed? And how are they to believe in him of whom they have never heard? And how are they to hear without a preacher? And how can men preach unless they are sent? . . . So faith comes from what is heard, and what is heard comes by the preaching of Christ. (Romans 10:13-15, 17)

But how are the church—and *each* of its members—to proclaim the good news of Jesus to others? Because the early church was so successful in its growth and outreach, it would be wise to seek the secret of its rapid growth.

Anglican missionary and writer Roland Allen has observed that there was no elaborate missionary plan or organization in the early church. Every Christian simply witnessed to Christ! Nor do we find in the New Testament repeated exhortations or reminders to Christians to spread their faith. Allen said that witnessing to their faith in Christ was the result of the early Christians' "natural instinct" and the Holy Spirit. It is natural to tell others about something good and important that has changed your life and has given it new purpose and meaning. However, Allen also comments,

> But in Christians there is more than this natural instinct. The Spirit of Christ is a Spirit who longs for, and strives after, the salvation of the souls of men, and that Spirit dwells in them. That Spirit converts the natural instinct into a longing for the conversion of others which is indeed divine in its source and character.[1]

Because of this natural and supernatural motivation of Christians to share their faith, the early church grew rapidly. Allen refers to it as the "spontaneous expansion of the church," because there was no human plan behind it—just Christians who freely told others about the good news they had received and who lived that good news in supportive and faith-filled local churches. These Christians did not look upon the church of Christ as an established organization or institution; they viewed it more as a "social movement" within Jewish and Roman society, whose goal was to bring others to the knowledge of Jesus Christ and of his love and saving plan for each person.

The early church's witness to Jesus was a result of more than just natural enthusiasm to tell others the good news. It was also a result of the Holy Spirit's enflaming this natural tendency with divine fire and giving the church wisdom from God about how to announce the gospel message. All this was as Jesus had promised. Hence, the rapid growth of early Christianity cannot be attributed to social and economic causes or psychological factors alone. Though many of these factors may have contributed to Christianity's growth and may help us to understand it better, the *root cause* of the rapid spread and growth of Christianity in the later Roman world was the Holy Spirit.

The Spirit gave the proclaimers boldness to announce the message, and wisdom to proclaim it rightly. He also opened the ears and hearts of the recipients of this message to hear and believe in Jesus and to join the community of believers, the church. At both the proclaiming and the receiving ends of the evangelization process, the Holy Spirit must act. Without him, there is no power and no conversion—no power of proclamation and no real conversion of heart. For this reason, Pope Paul VI called the Holy Spirit "the principal agent of evangelization: it is he who impels each individual to proclaim the gospel, and it is he who in the depths of consciences causes the word of salvation to be accepted and understood."[2]

On Evangelization in the Modern World

Pope Paul VI's 1975 apostolic letter *Evangelii Nuntiandi* (On Evangelization in the Modern World) is one of the most powerful documents on evangelization in the history of the Catholic church's missionary outreach. It is an expression of the pope's hope that pastors, theologians, and laypeople should study more thoroughly "the nature and manner of the Holy Spirit's action in evangelization today."

To understand evangelization, we must understand the work of the Holy Spirit—beginning with Christ, blossoming in the church at Pentecost, and continuing to our own time. Nothing could be clearer and more compelling than Pope Paul VI's own statement in *Evangelii Nuntiandi* that "evangelization will never be possible without the action of the Holy Spirit." The Holy Spirit's work of evangelization began with Christ. As Pope Paul explained,

> The Spirit descends on Jesus of Nazareth at the moment of his baptism when the voice of the Father—"This is my beloved Son with whom I am well pleased"—manifests in an external way the election of Jesus and his mission. Jesus is "led by the Spirit" to experience in the desert the decisive combat and the supreme test before beginning this mission. It is "in the power of the Spirit" that he returns to Galilee and begins his preaching at Nazareth, applying to himself the passage of Isaiah: "The Spirit of the Lord is upon me." And he proclaims: "Today this Scripture has been fulfilled." To the disciples whom he was about to send forth he says, breathing on them: "Receive the Holy Spirit."

The Holy Spirit continues to work through the apostles and through everyone who heard them speak:

> In fact, it is only after the coming of the Holy Spirit on the day of Pentecost that the apostles depart to all the ends of the earth in order to begin the great work of the church's evangelization. . . . Peter is filled with the Holy Spirit so that he can speak to the people about Jesus, the Son of God. Paul too is filled with the Holy Spirit before dedicating himself to his apostolic ministry, as is Stephen when he is chosen for the ministry of service and later on for the witness of blood. The Spirit, who causes Peter, Paul, and the Twelve to speak, and who inspires the words that they are to utter, also comes down "on those who heard the word."

It is, therefore, through the action of the Holy Spirit that the church has fulfilled and continues to fulfill its mission of evangelization:

> It is in the "consolation of the Holy Spirit" that the church increases. The Holy Spirit is the soul of the church. It is he who explains to the faithful the deep meaning of the teaching of Jesus and of his mystery. It is the Holy Spirit who, today just as at the beginning of the church, acts in every evangelizer who allows himself to be possessed and led by him. The Holy Spirit places on his lips the words which he could not find by himself and at the same time the Holy Spirit predisposes the soul of the hearer to be open and receptive to the good news and to the kingdom being proclaimed.

Without the Holy Spirit, evangelization would be impossible. As Pope Paul concluded,

> It must be said that the Holy Spirit is the principal agent of evangelization: it is he who impels each individual to proclaim the gospel, and it is he who in the depths of consciences causes the word of salvation to be accepted and understood.[3]

The Mission of the Redeemer

Following in the steps of his predecessor, Pope John Paul II also wrote a powerful encyclical letter on evangelism. Called *Redemptoris Missio* (The Mission of the Redeemer) the encyclical's purpose was to clarify the necessity, nature, and urgency of the church's missionary effort, echoing Vatican II's statement that "the pilgrim Church is missionary by her very nature."[4]

Such clarification is necessary because, in recent times, some Catholics have begun to wonder whether missionary activity is necessary or even appropriate today. Even some Catholics long involved with or dedicated to missionary outreach have raised questions about the need to convert non-Christians to Christ. Pope John Paul II responded clearly to these doubts and questions, insisting that "missionary activity is a matter for all Christians, for all dioceses, and parishes, Church institutions and associations" and inviting the church "to renew her missionary commitment. . . . For missionary activity renews the Church, revitalizes faith and Christian identity, and offers fresh enthusiasm and new incentive. Faith is strengthened when it is given away to others!"[5]

A church that does not share its faith with others stagnates and dies; indeed, the lack of zeal to proclaim the faith is already a sign of stagnation and impending spiritual death. A family that does not multiply will die out eventually. And, the church, too, will disappear if it does not effectively pass on its faith to others.

But why should Christians pass on their faith to others? Other people, after all, have beliefs that enable them to understand reality and lead good lives. In *Redemptoris Missio,* Pope John Paul II explained that evangelization is a gift or service to the world:

> But what moves me even more strongly to proclaim the urgency of missionary evangelization is the fact that it is the *primary service* which the Church can render to every individual and to all humanity in the modern world, a world which has experienced marvelous achievements but which seems to have lost its sense of ultimate realities and of existence itself.

"Christ the Redeemer," I wrote in my first encyclical, "fully reveals man to himself. . . . The person who wishes to understand himself thoroughly . . . must . . . draw near to Christ. . . . [The] Redemption that took place through the cross has definitively restored to man his dignity and given back meaning to his life in the world.[6]

Many Catholics are reluctant to evangelize, because they see it as "proselytizing," or interfering with another person's faith. Addressing these concerns, the pope wrote,

What is overlooked is that every person has the right to hear the Good News of the God who reveals and gives himself in Christ, so that each one can live out in its fullness his or her proper calling. This lofty reality is expressed in the words of Jesus to the Samaritan woman: "If you know the gift of God," and in the unconscious but ardent desire of the woman: "Sir, give me this water, that I may not thirst" (John 4:10, 15). The apostles, prompted by the Spirit, invited all to change their lives, to be converted and to be baptized.[7]

As Pope Paul VI explained in *Evangelii Nuntiandi,* the gift of the Holy Spirit to the disciples at Pentecost empowered them to spread the good news. In *Redemptoris Missio,* John Paul II added,

The coming of the Holy Spirit makes [the apostles] *witnesses* and *prophets* (cf. Acts 1:8; 2:17-18). It fills them with a serene courage which impels them to pass on to others their experience of Jesus and the hope which motivates them. The Spirit gives them the ability to bear witness to Jesus with "boldness." When the first evangelizers go down from Jerusalem, the Spirit becomes even more of a "guide," helping them to choose both those to whom they are to go and the places to which their missionary journey is to take them. The working of the Spirit is manifested particularly in the impetus given to the mission which, in accordance with Christ's words, spreads out from Jerusalem to all of Judea and Samaria, and to the farthest ends of the earth.[8]

The goal of evangelization is twofold: first, conversion, and then, creating and building the community of believers, the church. Pope John Paul II explained that conversion is a lifelong process of turning away from sin and toward God:

The proclamation of the word of God has *Christian conversion* as its aim: a complete and sincere adherence to Christ and his gospel through faith. . . . From the outset, conversion is expressed in faith which is total and radical, and which neither limits nor hinders God's gift. At the same time, it gives rise to a dynamic and lifelong process which demands a continual turning away from "life according to the flesh" to "life according to the Spirit" (cf. Romans 8:3-13).[9]

Prompted by the Spirit, the apostles invited everyone to be converted and baptized. Conversion and baptism are the means by which the Holy Spirit builds up the body of Christ, the church. As John Paul II explained,

The Spirit leads the company of believers to "form a community," to be the Church. After Peter's first proclamation on the day of Pentecost and the conversions that followed, the first community takes shape (cf. Acts 2:42-47; 4:32-35).[10]

Not only are individual Christians called to be evangelizers or witnesses to Christ, but the whole Christian community, by its life, worship, and activity is a powerful witness to the gospel:

> One of the central purposes of mission is to bring people together in hearing the gospel, in fraternal communion, in prayer and in the Eucharist. To live in "fraternal communion" (*koinonia*) means to be "of one heart and soul" (Acts 4:32), establishing fellowship from every point of view: human, spiritual and material. Indeed, a true Christian community is also committed to distributing earthly goods, so that no one is in want, and all can receive such goods "as they need" (cf. Acts 2:45; 4:35). . . . Even before activity, "mission" means witness and a way of life that shines out to others.[11]

In a sense, the ultimate work of the Holy Spirit in evangelization is to create a new community that is "eschatological"—a foretaste of the final projected kingdom of God. Pope Paul VI said in his letter on evangelization that the Holy Spirit is the goal of evangelization: "He alone stirs up the new creation, the new humanity of which evangelization is to be the result, with that unity in variety which evangelization wishes to achieve within the Christian community. Through the Holy Spirit the gospel penetrates to the heart of the world."[12]

The Motivation to Witness

How are the church and its members to once again become powerful witnesses to Christ in the world? The church has much practical wisdom about how to evangelize effectively and how to conduct missionary work. There are programs and workshops available to teach Catholics how to share their faith, and there are courses, schools, and seminaries to prepare people to do missionary work in foreign lands.

My observation, however, is that real and effective evangelization must begin with the work of the Holy Spirit in an individual's heart. Without the Spirit, there is no true motivation to evangelize. The scenario that frequently crosses my mind is someone—perhaps the pastor or a visiting missionary—addressing a typical Catholic parish on Sunday morning. The pastor or missionary tells the congregation about God's call to them to be evangelizers, witnesses of their faith to others in everyday life. Perhaps the speaker even quotes the powerful papal teachings on this subject. But to many of the hearers in the pews, the message is senseless or raises significant problems:

"Why do I have to tell people about my faith? It's a private matter, and embarrassing."

"I don't want to be a 'Bible-thumper.'"

"I don't want to become pushy about my beliefs."

And perhaps some of the more receptive will think, "Well, I guess if Father says I should, I'll give it a try sometime."

I observe that without the Holy Spirit stirring the heart, the *motivation* to evangelize is lacking. It remains external. Only the Holy Spirit can enable a person to really know God and his goodness as well as his love for us in Jesus Christ. Only the Holy Spirit can give people a fervent *desire*, arising from within, to tell others about God and the beauty and truth of their faith. Pope Paul VI expressed this pointedly:

> Techniques of evangelization are good, but even the most advanced ones could not replace the gentle action of the Spirit. The most perfect preparation of the evangelizer has no effect without the Holy Spirit.

Without the Holy Spirit the most convincing dialectic has no power over the heart of man. Without him the most highly developed schemas resting on a sociological or psychological basis are quickly seen to be quite valueless.[13]

The Holy Spirit Makes the Difference

The Catholic Church teaches a thorough and inspiring doctrine of evangelization and exhorts its members to witness to their faith. But how many Catholics actually do it? Author Peter Kreeft notes that what is missing among so many Christians today is the same thing that St. Paul found missing in the early churches:

When Paul visits the church in Ephesus (Acts 19), he notices something missing—I think he would notice exactly the same thing in most of our churches and preach the same sermon—and he asks them, "Did you receive the Holy Spirit when you believed?" (Acts 19:2). Why would he ask that unless he saw a power shortage? Why did twelve fishermen convert the world, and why are half a billion Christians unable to repeat the feat? The Spirit makes the difference.[14]

The Spirit makes the difference. I propose that we begin to restore evangelization and missionary fervor in the Catholic Church by constant prayer for a renewed outpouring of the Holy Spirit, as at Pentecost. This, of course, is not a new proposal. The church teaches us to pray: "Come Holy Spirit, fill the hearts of your faithful, and enkindle in them the fire of your love."

It is no coincidence that the Catholics who most actively witness to their faith are generally those who have had some experience of the Holy Spirit touching and transforming their lives. However, this work of the Spirit needs to be constantly renewed and refreshed in each Christian. Every Christian receives the Holy Spirit in baptism, and Catholics are blessed with a special sacrament, confirmation, for the deepening of the gift of the Holy Spirit to enable us to witness to Christ and to live as committed adult Christians in the world.

Christians should implore God for the release of this grace of the Holy Spirit in their lives. Without it, it is impossible to live as true Christians, fulfilling Jesus' call to follow him and to be his witnesses. Thus, evangelization begins with *prayer,* prayer for the empowering grace of the Holy Spirit. Those who do not desire to share their faith should pray for the Holy Spirit to implant or to stir up this desire! Those who have fears and reservations that are obstacles to their involvement should ask the Holy Spirit to conquer them.

This is not to say that *all* we need is the Holy Spirit in order to witness to Christ effectively. Some people may need help and counsel to overcome obstacles or to heal past hurts. We all need encouragement from each other, and sometimes advice, which is the proper task of the Christian community. (Do the people in your parish encourage you to witness to Christ or provide advice on how it might be done, or better done, in your circumstances?)

Christians also need instruction on what to say and how to answer questions that arise. Witness based purely on personal experience is narrow and even possibly dangerous. Once the Holy Spirit provides the desire or zeal to evangelize, then the thirst for guidance or instruction usually follows. Roland Allen comments,

> Given spontaneous zeal we can direct it by instruction. Aquila could teach Apollos the way of God

more perfectly. . . . All religious experience demands doctrine for its proper statement and explanation.[15]

Allen explains that when people have a fervent desire to witness to their faith, they receive teaching with joy. They know their need for instruction to explain their faith effectively, and their spiritual experience produces a hunger to know more about God and the truth he has revealed. Doctrinal instruction is important, but in order to witness to their faith, Christians must first have the desire to evangelize, which is a gift enkindled in our hearts by the Holy Spirit.

The Spirituality of the Witness

Even with zeal and information, effective evangelization requires a constantly nourished spirituality. Pope John Paul II explained that the spirituality of the evangelizer or missionary must be characterized by docility:

This spirituality is expressed first of all by a life of complete docility to the Spirit. It commits us to being molded from within by the Spirit, so that we may become ever more like Christ. It is not possible to bear witness to Christ without reflecting his image, which is made alive in us by grace and the power of the Spirit. This docility then commits us to receive the gifts of fortitude and discernment, which are essential elements of missionary spirituality.[16]

What are some of the common marks of the spiritual life of the evangelist? The missionary must be a "contemplative in action" and "a person of the Beatitudes," said Pope John Paul II. Other specific characteristics he listed include

114

- intimate communion with Christ;
- self-renunciation and "a poverty which sets him free for the gospel";
- apostolic charity: the heart of Christ the Good Shepherd;
- hearts aflame with a "zeal and burning love" for souls;
- love for the church;
- commitment to holiness—a "new ardor for holiness"—even before advanced study and updated pastoral techniques.[17]

Many of John Paul II's reflections echo the words of Pope Paul VI, who also had much to say about the spirituality of those who evangelize. For example, he insisted that evangelizing zeal must spring from true holiness of life, "which is nourished by prayer and above all by love for the Eucharist."[19] Like all the other characteristics mentioned above, that too is a work of the Holy Spirit in the faithful.

Pope Paul VI argued that the spiritual void in the modern world can only be filled by the witness of people who know God personally. Calling to mind such great evangelistic saints as St. Dominic, St. Francis of Assisi, and St. Clare, he proclaimed,

> The world calls for and expects from us simplicity of life, the spirit of prayer, charity towards all, especially towards the lowly and the poor, obedience and humility, detachment and self-sacrifice. Without this mark of holiness, our word will have difficulty in touching the heart of modern man. It risks being vain and sterile.[18]

Paul VI also stressed the need to restore Christian unity:

> As evangelizers, we must offer Christ's faithful not the image of people divided and separated by unedi-

fying quarrels, but the image of people who are mature in faith and capable of finding a meeting-point beyond the real tensions, thanks to a shared, sincere and disinterested search for truth. Yes, the destiny of evangelization is certainly bound up with the witness of unity given by the church. This is a source of responsibility and also of comfort.[19]

Pope Paul VI discusses other key elements of evangelization, including a firm adherence to the truth and genuine love of those who are being addressed. But, as he saw it, the greatest need of evangelizers today is *fervor.*

It would be useful if every Christian and every evangelizer were to pray about the following thought: men can gain salvation also in other ways, by God's mercy, even though we do not preach the gospel to them; but as for us, can we gain salvation if through negligence or fear or shame . . . we fail to preach it? . . . Let us therefore preserve our fervor of spirit. . . . May [evangelizing] mean for us—as it did for John the Baptist, for Peter and Paul, for the other apostles and for a multitude of splendid evangelizers all through the church's history—an interior enthusiasm that nobody and nothing can quench. May it be the great joy of our consecrated lives. And may the world of our time, which is searching, sometimes with anguish, sometimes with hope, be enabled to receive the Good News . . . from ministers of the gospel whose lives glow with fervor, who have first received the joy of Christ, and who are willing to risk their lives so that the kingdom may be proclaimed and the church established in the midst of the world."[20]

This fervor to spread the gospel of Jesus Christ is not something the Christian creates or "manufactures": it is a gift of the Holy Spirit. Let us ask the Holy Spirit to fill us with fervor to witness to Christ and to "enkindle in us the fire of his love."

CHAPTER SEVEN

Building the Church

A typical Catholic parish is composed of an active, often overworked, pastor and his associates, who carry on the work of running the parish with the help of a core of dedicated religious and laity. Decisions about what the parish does are made in a practical, realistic way by the pastor and sometimes by the other parish staff and the pastoral (parish) council. The decisions must be shown to be realistic, affordable (or profit-producing), and likely to be accepted by most members of the parish. An active parish requires a lot of vision, dedication, and hard work to build up the body of Christ.

This approach to parish life is not necessarily incorrect; an active, successful parish involves good planning and hard work. However, we must always be seeking to find and implement *God's* plan for the life and operation of the church, which, after all, is his idea and his creation.

It is easy to make building up the church into *our* project: planned by our own wisdom and intelligence and executed by our own strength and energy. (This is the basis of the Pelagian heresy: the belief that we can save ourselves and do good by our own efforts apart from God's grace.) And, yet, as the first verse of Psalm 127 reminds us, "Unless the Lord builds the house they who build it labor in vain."

The first chapter of the central document of the Second Vatican Council, *Lumen Gentium* (The Dogmatic Constitution on the Church), speaks of the "mystery" of the church. The church is a mystery, because it is, like Christ its founder, a union of both divine and human elements. Human energy and intelligence *are* needed to guide and advance the king-dom of God on earth, but those gifts must be supplemented by and conformed to the strength and wisdom of God. Otherwise, the church will fail or become just another human organization, indistinguishable from other charitable or humanitarian groups.

Jesus Christ and his Father have sent the Holy Spirit so that God's church might be planned and built up according to *God's* own purposes and by his strength. This chapter will explore how the church is to be built or "built up" in God's plan through the Holy Spirit.

The premise upon which this chapter is based is that the gifts of the Holy Spirit are a normal part of Christian life. They are usually first received when the Holy Spirit is first received—through the sacraments of initiation. When the Holy Spirit is poured out into a person at baptism, and in a new way at confirmation, the Spirit not only dwells within that person but comes bearing gifts and graces. Some of these graces are given to all who receive the sacrament, some are gifts and graces given to particular persons as God wills. Building up the church requires that all Christians desire and identify the Spirit's gifts, for, as Catholic scholars George Montague and Kilian McDonnell explain,

As these gifts are sought (1 Corinthians 14:1) and discerned (1 Thessalonians 5:19-21), they empower members to create that communion which the Church is meant to be and to proclaim the Church's message of love, justice and peace to the world. This life in the Holy Spirit is not, therefore, one spirituality among others in the Church. It is the spirituality of the Church.[1]

Guidance in the Life of the Church

The first aspect of the Holy Spirit's work in building the church is to guide it in its life and decisions. I was impressed by the story of Fr. Michael Scanlan, former president of Franciscan University of Steubenville. In 1974, when he was first installed as president, Fr. Scanlan used to spend most of each morning in prayer before he came into the office to do the day's business. He explained that there was no use coming into the office if he didn't know what God wanted him to do, and so he would "wait on God" in prayer until he received some sense of God's direction. Then he would come to work and act on what he had discerned from his prayer.

From the very beginning, the church has relied on the Holy Spirit's guidance. Jesus didn't give his apostles a detailed blueprint of how they were to build the church. He just told them that they were to teach, forgive sins, proclaim the gospel, make disciples of all nations, heal, expel demons in his name, and so on.

But the "how, when, and where" of the apostles' mission was apparently left unspecified by Jesus. Even after Jesus' first appearance following his resurrection, it seems that the apostles did not know quite what to do, so they stayed around the "upper room" or went fishing in Galilee.

The outpouring of the Holy Spirit at Pentecost provided the apostles and the early church not only with the power but also with the practical direction that they needed. There are many examples of the Holy Spirit's guidance in the Acts of the Apostles. When Philip saw the Ethiopian treasury minister riding down the desert road from Jerusalem to Gaza, "the Spirit said to Philip, 'Go up and join this chariot'" (Acts 8:29). Philip ended up converting and baptizing this man and "the Spirit of the Lord caught up Philip; and the eunuch saw him no more, and went on his way rejoicing. But Philip was found at Azotus, and passing on he preached the gospel to all the towns till he came to Caesarea" (Acts 8:39-40).

The Holy Spirit also instructed Peter to accompany the three men seeking him to Cornelius' house, where he first baptized gentiles (see Acts 10:19; 11:12). The ministry of St. Paul is replete with instances of the Holy Spirit's selecting him for a certain task and then guiding him specifically where he is to go next (see, for example, Acts 13:2-9; 16:6-7; 20:22-23).

It appears that the Holy Spirit provided the primitive church with continual guidance, and even a variety of different types of guidance. Some of these included practical guidance about *where* to go to witness to Christ and *whom* to set apart for a particular ministry. At other times that guidance might be called *discernment:* testing *what* is of God and what is not (see Acts 13:9-10). This "discernment of spirits" is quite important in the life of the church, because in every age false teachings and teachers arise and deceive many (see 2 Timothy 4:3-4; 2 Peter 2:1-3). So sacred Scripture instructs Christians to "test the spirits" (1 John 4:1) and "hold fast what is good" (1 Thessalonians 5:21). Indeed, St. Paul speaks of "the ability to distinguish between spirits" as a particular gift of the Holy Spirit (see 1 Corinthians 12:10).

To build the church or the kingdom of God, we need God's guidance and instruction, and we need it every day in practical matters. "What am I to do?" "Who should I speak to and encourage in the faith today?" "Is what I am reading or viewing right now witnessing to the lordship of Jesus Christ, or is it opposed to Christ and his teaching?" These judgments are not always simple. In all cases, Christians need the Holy Spirit to guide us to do what is most pleasing to God and what will advance his kingdom most effectively.

There is a danger that the seeking of this guidance could be exaggerated and lead to a sort of "illuminism"—expecting God to reveal in a direct, supernatural way everything a person is to do. This sort of guidance can properly be sought by asking the Holy Spirit at the beginning of each day to direct one in all the day's decisions, interactions, and personal encounters. The *Catechism* notes that "the Church invites us to call upon the Holy Spirit every day, especially at the beginning and the end of every important action" (2670). During the day, we could perhaps pray, "Come, Holy Spirit" when particular help or guidance is needed. We could then proceed to act according to our best judgment or "sense" of what is best or the right thing to do, trusting that the Spirit will guide us.

More important decisions or discernments will require more specific, ongoing prayer for God's guidance through the Holy Spirit. This might include seeking guidance concerning a vocation or marriage partner; how to be a good parent (in general, or in a certain difficult situation); how to conduct oneself at work or in particular projects, decisions, or relationships at work; and so on. The crucial thing to remember is that God cares about our lives and about all the difficulties that confront and concern us. The Holy Spirit has been given to Christians to guide us in all these things.

God has also sent the Holy Spirit to us because he desires to establish his kingdom in us and through us. The documents of Vatican II state that all Christ's faithful people share in the kingship of Jesus—which means that while we are on earth we carry on Jesus' mission of proclaiming and establishing God's reign or kingdom. This task requires both the power and the guidance of the Holy Spirit. The section on the "kingly" role of the laity in *Lumen Gentium* says that the laity establish the kingdom of God, first, by "overcoming the reign of sin in themselves," second, by "bringing their brethren to that King, whom to serve is to reign," and finally, by "spreading the values of the kingdom of God in the world, the kingdom of truth and life, the kingdom of holiness and grace, the kingdom of justice, love, and peace . . . ordering . . . the whole of creation to the praise of God."[2] What enables the Christian to carry out those high-sounding words in daily life, decisions, and actions is the Holy Spirit. The Spirit of God gives us the gift of fortitude, or courage, to act according to God's will, and the practical guidance to discern what would best promote God's kingdom in ourselves, others, and the world in each situation.

It should be noted once again that the guidance of the Holy Spirit in the lives of Christians is not illuminism or direct private revelation of all the truths and principles of the gospel, or of those that flow from it. In other words, reliable guidance of the Holy Spirit requires that a person know the true doctrine taught by the church. The Holy Spirit cannot lead a person to do something that violates the truth, and usually the truth must be studied to be known.

Recognition of the truth, as we have seen, is another work of the Holy Spirit; it can lead a person, for example, to recognize the truth of the Bible or of authentic church teaching. The Holy Spirit, then, enables a person to *grow* in understanding of this truth and teaching, so that he or she may live this teaching, share it with others, and, with the Holy Spirit's guidance, make decisions based on truth rather than on half-truth or error.

Also, the Holy Spirit often guides us by means of the advice and counsel of others. Far from providing only direct personal guidance, God has made us part of the body of Christ, "members of one another," as St. Paul says, so that Christians can help one another to discern and encourage one another to do God's will. Seeking wise and mature counsel, as well as being open to God's "speaking" through *anyone* (after all, he spoke to Balaam through his donkey: see Numbers 22), is an important way of receiving guidance and direction. The Holy Spirit often speaks to us through others if we are open and receptive to this guidance.

Gifts of the Spirit

The second major aspect of the Holy Spirit's work to build the church and advance God's kingdom is the outpouring of various gifts (*charismata,* in Greek). There are two different biblical sources for what are called the gifts of Holy Spirit. The first source is Isaiah 11:2. Catholics have traditionally associated this list—wisdom, understanding, counsel, knowledge, fortitude, piety, and fear of the Lord—as the seven gifts of the Spirit that are given in a new way by Christ through the sacrament of confirmation. This makes sense, because Isaiah understands these as particular gifts that will be possessed in fullness by the long-awaited Messiah and Savior of Israel (Cf. *Catechism of the Catholic Church,* 712, 1303).

Christ is the model of these gifts, because through the Spirit he possessed them in their fullness. They are much like the "fruit of the Spirit" listed by St. Paul in his letter to the Galatians: love, joy, peace, patience, goodness, kindness, gentleness, generosity, and self-control (Cf. *Catechism,* 736, 1832). These are all marks of the character of a Christian as he or she is more fully conformed to the image of Christ. All the Isaian gifts of the Spirit are offered to all Christians, especially in the sacraments. Yet, they gradually grow to varying degrees in each Christian, like fruit on a tree, as they are sought in prayer and the sacraments and cultivated through action and practice. Through the Holy Spirit, we grow to become people who are wise, understanding, reverent, and God-fearing.

The other biblical source for the gifts of the Holy Spirit is the Pauline literature of the New Testament. Here, the workings of the Spirit are called gifts (*charismata*) or manifestations of the Spirit (*pneumatika*). They are listed in 1 Corinthians 12:8-10, 28; Romans 12:6-8, and Ephesians 4:11. The *Catechism* refers to them simply as charisms (799–801).

These gifts include apostleship, prophecy, teaching, working miracles, administration, speaking in tongues (glossolalia), the word of wisdom, the word of knowledge, faith, healing, discernment of spirits, interpretation of tongues, evangelism, pastoring, acts of mercy, service, exhortation, giving aid, and even giving money! None of these lists is *exhaustive;* the implication is that there is a wide (perhaps even infinite) variety of gifts.

Here is a brief explanation of some of the gifts of the Spirit mentioned by St. Paul:

The utterance, or *word of wisdom,* is a special insight given by the Holy Spirit in a particular situation for the advancement of the kingdom of God. It is the fulfillment of Jesus' promise to his disciples that he would give them wisdom "which none of your adversaries will be able to withstand or contradict" (Luke 21:15). The word of wisdom is an application of the gospel to a new situation in such a way that its meaning is preserved, though its formulation may be somewhat different. It can also refer to a supernatural revelation of the thoughts of another person or persons.

Faith as a gift of the Spirit is not exactly the same as the theological virtue. It is the type of extraordinary faith "so as to remove mountains" (see Matthew 17:20; 1 Corinthians 13:2), by which miracles and mighty works are performed in the Lord's name.

The *gifts of healing* refer not only to physical healing but to any restoration of health to a person's body, soul, or spirit. The book of Acts records many such instances of the gifts of healing among the apostles (see, for example, Acts 3:6-10; 5:16; 19:11-12). Gifts of healing are given to members of the body of Christ so that human diseases and disabilities of every kind—organic and inorganic, psychological as well as physical—can be healed through the direct action of Jesus Christ and the ministry of the Christian.

The *working of miracles* is the Spirit's gift of performing other extraordinary signs of the power of God. These include healing the sick and raising the dead (see Acts; 26:8) and performing "nature miracles" (see Acts 16:26; 28:3-6).

The gift of *prophecy* does not in essence have to do with predicting the future. It is a gift by which God speaks a message to an individual, a group, or an entire Christian community. It may or may not be accompanied by an action illuminating the spoken word.

Discernment of spirits is that gift whereby Christians are able to judge whether something—an event, a proposal, an utterance—is from the Holy Spirit of God, from the human spirit of man, or from evil spirits. It may therefore refer to the gift given by the Spirit to the Christian community to discern what prophecies or teachings actually are from God, or it may refer to a gift given to individuals to detect when an evil or demonic spirit is present (Cf. *Catechism*, 801).

The gift of *tongues (glossolalia)* actually may refer to either one of two distinct gifts of the Holy Spirit. The first is glossolalia as a *prayer gift,* by which an individual is enabled to pray or sing aloud or quietly in a language unknown to the person. The recipient of this prayer gift is enabled to praise and thank God, to grieve, intercede, or simply cry out to God in a "strange tongue" that may be either known or unknown to any human being (the tongues of angels or of men, as St. Paul puts it).

Glossolalia may also be a prophecy spoken aloud in an unknown language, a "word from God" to another person or to the church community. Paul praises this type of glossolalia in particular because it builds up the entire church, not just the individual believer possessing the gift. It is a word from God addressed to the local community.

However, this gift is useless unless it is interpreted for the community by someone with the gift of *interpretation of tongues*. And so, when someone addressed the assembled community with a "prophetic" gift of tongues, St. Paul required that the message be interpreted (see 1 Corinthians 14:27). Interpretation probably did not mean literal translation of the message in tongues, but rather a spiritual gift of discerning the meaning of the word that God was addressing to the community, and then speaking it in understandable language.

Paul realized how important it was to understand the meaning of messages spoken in tongues; this impelled him to urge those who spoke in tongues to "pray for the power to interpret" (1 Corinthians 14:13), so that the whole body might benefit more fully from these messages. This encouragement was not only for the givers of the messages, however. Others could also provide the interpretation (see 1 Corinthians 12:10; 14:26).

Many of these charisms are commonly known as "word gifts," gifts of the Spirit that build up the body of Christ through an inspired word or words from God of one type or another, such as prophecy or word of wisdom. Other Pauline gifts, such as healing and miracles, involve prayer and action. St. Paul lists a number of gifts of the Spirit that do not require explanation: teaching and service to others are two examples.

It is tragic that charisms have been a source of contention in the church today, for they are God's gift to unify and build up his church. As the *Catechism of the Catholic Church* teaches, charisms are to be valued:

> Charisms are to be accepted with gratitude by the person who receives them and by all members of the Church as well. They are a wonderfully rich grace for the apostolic vitality and for the holiness of the entire Body of Christ, provided they really are genuine gifts of the Holy Spirit and are used in full conformity with authentic promptings of this same Spirit that is, in keeping with charity, the true measure of all charisms. (800)

Further, the fact that *each* Christian has a charism for use in the church and the world is a source of the dignity of the Christian. There are no "ungifted" people or ones who are merely dependent on others. The unity of the church is built as we come to recognize each other's gifts and value them instead of seeing ourselves as in competition with each other over who has the greater gift (or gifts). The gifts then lead to the glory and praise of God, who is their source and who distributes them freely to all as he wills. The gifts of the Holy Spirit lead us to rely on God's grace in all things, and to the awareness that all our accomplishments are really his gifts. They also lead us to a greater awareness of the transcendent nature of the church, as we yield to, and foster the use of, gifts such as prophecy, healing, discernment, and even speaking in tongues.

Let us follow the teaching of the Second Vatican Council as expressed in the *Catechism*, which urges us to accept the charisms—both those given to us and those given to others—with gratitude, as they make us "fit and ready to undertake various tasks and offices for the renewal and building up of the Church" (798).

What distinguishes the Pauline gifts of the Spirit from the gifts of the Messiah in Isaiah? First, not everyone possesses or will possess all the Pauline gifts. They are explicitly given by God for the service or building up of the community of the church, and so it is not necessary for all to possess the same gifts or all the gifts. In fact, it is precisely because different people have different gifts that the church is built up in strength and unity by its different members.

Since no Christian possesses all or even most of the gifts, the followers of Christ must learn to rely on each other and contribute to one another. Christians are interdependent, not independent, because the gifts God has given them are complementary. St. Paul uses the analogy of the human body to explain, "As it is, there are many parts, yet one body. The eye cannot say to the hand, 'I have no need of you,' nor again the head to the feet, 'I have no need of you'" (1 Corinthians 12:20-21).

The gifts of the Spirit listed by St. Paul often benefit the individual Christian in his or her spiritual growth, but the most important or valuable gifts, according to St. Paul, are those that strengthen others in the body of Christ. That is why prophecy is seen by St. Paul as objectively more important than praying in tongues. St. Paul even urges Christians to "earnestly desire the spiritual gifts, especially that you may prophesy":

> For one who speaks in a tongue speaks not to men but to God; for no one understands him, but he utters mysteries of the Spirit. On the other hand, he who prophesies speaks to men for their upbuilding and encouragement and consolation. . . . So with yourselves; since you are eager for manifestations of the Spirit, strive to excel in building up the church. (1 Corinthians 14:2-3, 12)

The members of the early church had some difficulty understanding the meaning and purpose of the spiritual gifts. It is not surprising, then, that the gifts or charisms of the Holy Spirit are widely misunderstood today by Catholics and many other Christians. Dispelling these misconceptions will lead us to a better appreciation for the charisms and show us how they apply to our lives as twenty-first-century Christians.

Only for the Few?

The first misunderstanding is that spiritual gifts are unusual or extraordinary, possessed by only a chosen few. But St. Paul's explanation of the charisms indicates just the opposite: *every* Christian possesses some (at *least* one) charism or spiritual gift:

> *To each* is given the manifestation of the Spirit for the common good. To one is given through the Spirit the utterance of wisdom, and to another the utterance of knowledge according to the same Spirit, to another faith by the same Spirit, to another gifts of healing by the one Spirit, to another the working of miracles, to another prophecy, to another the ability to distinguish between spirits, to another various kinds of tongues, to another the interpretation of tongues. All these are inspired by one and the same Spirit, who apportions *to each one individually* as he wills. (1 Corinthians 12:7-11, emphasis mine)

St. Paul states that *each* Christian is given some manifestation—gift, or gifts—of the Spirit. Thus, it would be true to say that every Christian is "charismatic." Every person has something—some gift of God—to contribute to the building of God's kingdom.

Tools, Not Toys

Why does God grant gifts of the Spirit to all his people? The second common misunderstanding about the charisms is that they are given to meet some people's need for an emotional experience to keep them going in the Christian life. The charisms, according to this misperception, satisfy our human desire for the sensational, for consolation, or for proof of God's existence. Like miracles, they confirm that God is alive and active for those who cannot accept this reality through faith.

St. Paul's explanation of why God bestows the gifts of the Holy Spirit has nothing to do with emotions. The charisms are not toys to amuse or entertain us or simply to confirm our faith. They are God's essential tools for strengthening his body, the church: "To each is given the manifestation of the Spirit *for the common good*" (1 Corinthians 12:7, emphasis mine). Often St. Paul uses the words "edification" or "edify" ("building up" or "build up") to explain why the gifts of the Spirit are given:

> When you come together, each one has a hymn, a lesson, a revelation, a tongue, or an interpretation. Let all things be done for edification. (1 Corinthians 14:26)

> And his gifts were that some should be apostles, some prophets, some evangelists, some pastors and teachers, for the equipment of the saints, for the work of ministry, for building up the body of Christ.
> (Ephesians 4:11-12)

The gifts of the Spirit are the "equipment" that Christians need to carry out the service or ministry of the church to itself and others. That should not surprise us. If the church were a purely human reality, it could be built and led by purely human talents and abilities. But because the church is also a spiritual reality, sharing in God's own nature, it must be built up and led by divine or spiritual gifts. (These spiritual gifts may, in some cases, build upon human talents and abilities, but often they are more obviously a sovereign work or gift of God.) It is for building the church that Christians are given the tools of the gifts of the Holy Spirit, as Pope John Paul II explains in his teaching about the laity:

> Whether they be exceptional and great or simple and ordinary, the charisms are graces of the Holy Spirit that have, directly or indirectly, a usefulness for the ecclesiastical community, ordered as they are to the building up of the Church, to the well-being of humanity and to the needs of the world. Even in our own times there is no lack of a fruitful manifestation of various charisms among the faithful, women and men.[3]

These charisms, the gifts of the Holy Spirit, are so important in the life of the church and of each Christian that the Second Vatican Council taught that they are one of three primary ways that God leads his people to holiness, along with the sacraments and the ordained ministry.[4]

Charism and Institution

Placing the spiritual gifts on the same level as the sacrament and the ordained ministry of the church has lead to a third common misunderstanding: that there is some opposition or tension between the charismatic gifts and the ministry of the ordained members or hierarchy of the church. There has been much written about the relationship between "charism" and "institution" illustrating that the relationship between the charisms and the hierarchy of the church is actually interdependent and complementary. From that literature, I would draw the following conclusions:

- The "offices," or ordained ministries, of the church are based on charisms.
- Charisms are a principal source of the life and dynamism of the "institutional church."
- Those who have the charisms of leadership are gifted to discern and regulate the decisions and activities of the other members of the church.

As Fr. Karl Rahner wrote, there is no "opposition or hostility between the official institutions of the church on the one hand and the charismatic elements on the other."[5] Jesus himself imparted to the church some structure, or institutional form, when he selected and prepared the apostles to teach and govern his people. Later, the Holy Spirit led the primitive church to appoint other elders, such as the deacons or servants, to provide other official services (see Acts 6).

These different roles of servant leadership came to be called the hierarchy. Yet, we must remember that these offices are based on charisms or gifts given to the officeholders to carry out their various tasks of service to the church. Some scholars speak of the charisms as institutional, but it is more accurate to say that the persons possessing certain charisms of leadership assume particular roles (or offices) within the church. These persons take their place in the institution, or hierarchy, of church leadership according to the gifts or charisms they have been given.

Yet, we must also remember that those who are ordained and hold office in the church do not possess *all* the charisms; rather, *all* members of this institution, the church, possess particular gifts of the Holy Spirit for building up Christ's body. And they are to use them freely for the service of God's people.

As St. Thomas Aquinas taught, the charisms are not given to God's people by or through the hierarchy, but they are *gratia gratis datae*—graces freely given by God. Some people are given the gift to be apostles, some prophets, some pastors and teachers, and so on (see 1 Corinthians 12:28ff). Fr. Karl Rahner once called the charisms the *"motive* force" in the institutional church. The gifts of the Holy Spirit empower the church (and each person in it) to fulfill its mission in God's plan. The ordained leaders are chosen because God has freely given them particular gifts suited to their office, and other gifts through their ordination. God gives ordained leaders the particular gifts and graces that they need to carry out their office of service.

The ordained leaders of the church (especially the bishops, but also other pastors) do have a particular ministry with regard to the charisms of the other members of the church. One of their gifts, as well as the commission of their office, is to discern or "test" the charisms of members of the church and to *order* these gifts in some way so that they will fulfill most perfectly their purpose: to build up the whole church.

I find the analogy of the orchestra conductor to be most helpful: the conductor has not given the members of the orchestra their musical gifts and talents (that comes from God), but he has been given the gift to discern whether someone has the gift to play in the orchestra, and to "conduct" or order how the musicians use their gifts together to produce harmony and beautiful music. The conductor would be foolish to think that he could produce the music by himself, for he does not have all the gifts (or at least he could not exercise them—play them—all at once). So he uses *his* power, the gift to lead and conduct the orchestra to bring forth the best from all its members.

At times, this may mean that the pastors of the church have to correct abuses in the use of the spiritual gifts. However, the dominant attitude of pastors must be a desire to encourage and foster these gifts and not to "quench the Spirit" (1 Thessalonians 5:19).

How the hierarchy and the faithful are to approach the charisms was expressed simply and directly by the Second Vatican Council. In summary, the council taught that the gifts of the Holy Spirit "are to be received with thanksgiving and consolation" and that the faithful have the "the right and duty" of exercising even the most ordinary spiritual gifts for the good of the church in the freedom of the Holy Spirit. The role of the pastors is to test these gifts—not to stifle or quench them, but to promote and direct them for the good of the whole church.[6]

We might say that the institutional aspect of the church *exists* to foster and encourage the charisms and the free working of the Holy Spirit, and that the charisms support and enliven the church as an organized social institution. God freely grants spiritual gifts to all the members of the church as he sees fit and calls those who are "gifted" (that is, the "charismatics," meaning all Christians) to use their gifts to build up the church, lest they imitate the timid man in Jesus' parable who buried his talent and was rebuked for it. The church is open to the rule of Christ through his Spirit. The ordained pastors of the church (the hierarchy) are to support God's action in the church. As Pope Benedict XVI wrote before he assumed the papacy,

> Our task—the task of the office-holders in the church and of theologians—is to keep the door open to them [those in the new "charismatic" movements], to prepare room for them.[7]

The saints are probably the best example of how God uses figures outside of the hierarchy to strengthen and enliven the church. Pope Pius XII, in his encyclical *Mystici Corporis Christi,* noted that God governs his church both through his guidance of the hierarchy and through women and men of outstanding sanctity with particular charisms or gifts for the church. Fr. Karl Rahner provides a few excellent examples:

> Anthony the Hermit, Benedict, Francis of Assisi, Catherine of Siena, Margaret Mary Alacoque, Theresa of the child Jesus and many others have all been of irreplaceable importance for the history of the church and for the church herself in their function of direct receptors of the impulses of the Spirit."[8]

Charisms for Today's Church

Another common misconception about the charisms is that they were widely distributed in the primitive church to empower her for her initial growth and mission but became unnecessary afterward—like the huge rockets of a space vehicle that fall away after they have fulfilled their purpose of getting the vehicle into orbit. But was the great diversity of charisms that St. Paul writes about *just* intended for the primitive church?

This cannot be the case, as we see from the teaching of the Second Vatican Council and of recent popes. Speaking of the importance of spiritual gifts in the church today, Fr. Karl Rahner wrote,

> The charismatic element was not merely bestowed in order to facilitate the initial stages of the church's life. . . . Since then any spontaneous manifestations of the charismatic were all too easily suspected of being "enthusiasm," and there was an exaggerated

tendency to recognize the charismatic as manifested in certain specific historic forms which in fact are out of date. Against this view it is in fact that the very nature of the charismatic [is] an essential trait inherent in the church.[9]

Pope Paul VI gave a pastoral reflection in which he commented on the "effusion" or "rain" of charisms in the church's recent history:

When the Holy Spirit comes, he grants gifts. We already know of the seven gifts of the Holy Spirit, but he also gives other gifts . . . called charisms. What is the meaning of "charism"? It means "gift." It means a grace. They are particular graces given to one person or another, in order to do good. One receives the charism of wisdom in order to become a teacher, and another receives the gift of miracles in order to perform deeds which, through wonder and admiration, call others to the faith.[10]

Pope John Paul II also spoke of the fruitfulness of the charisms in the church today and encouraged openness to them:

The Second Vatican Council reserved special attention for the multiform action of the Spirit in the history of salvation. . . . The council pointed out the Holy Spirit's action in each of the faithful, whom he stimulates to a courageous apostolic testimony, strengthening them by means of the sacraments and enriching them with "special graces. . . . By these gifts he makes them fit and ready to undertake the various tasks or offices advantageous for the renewal and building up of the Church" (*Lumen Gentium*, no. 12).[11]

A Matter of Discernment

But what of someone who doesn't feel that he or she has received any spiritual gifts. It would be easy, in that case, to write off the charisms as mere "natural" talents, or to see them as peripheral, unnecessary, enthusiastic emotionalism, over-spiritual, or simply as "bunk." St. Paul apparently encountered some of these attitudes. He wrote the Corinthians,

> The unspiritual man does not receive the gifts of the Spirit of God for they are folly to him, and he is not able to understand them because they are spiritually discerned. The spiritual man judges all things, but is himself judged by no one. "For who has known the mind of the Lord so as to instruct him?" But we have the mind of Christ. (1 Corinthians 2:14-16)

The gifts of the Spirit cannot be dismissed as elitist or the product of emotions, nor can they be reduced to nothing more than natural talent. With the "mind of Christ," we understand that God has granted each person one or more gifts for the building up of the church. Some of these *appear* to us to be merely natural talents, such as organizational gifts of administration or leadership gifts of teaching or pastoring others.

Catholics have always said that "grace builds on nature"; it is also true, with regard to the spiritual gifts, that "nature" is to some degree built on grace. That is, what may appear to us to be "natural" gifts or talents are really gifts or graces that God has given. All this illustrates what many noted Catholic theologians have been saying in recent times: that drawing a sharp, clear division between the natural and the supernatural is not possible. All creation flows from and reflects or expresses the fullness and grace of God.

The "spiritual" person knows this. Some gifts of the Holy Spirit appear more purely spiritual—among them, prophecy, speaking in tongues, and interpretation of tongues. Other gifts we consider natural—service or administration, for example—but they also come from God as his gifts through the Holy Spirit. This becomes clear as Christians grow in looking at reality with eyes of faith, that is, with belief in the source of all good things in God.

St. Paul provides a sound pastoral perspective for looking at ourselves to discover the gifts that God has given us for his glory and for the service of others. In his Letter to the Romans, he wrote,

> For by the grace given to me I bid every one among you not to think of himself more highly than he ought to think, but to think with sober judgment, each according to the measure of faith which God has assigned him.
>
> For as in one body we have many members, and all the members do not have the same function, so we, though many, are one body in Christ, and individually members of one another.
>
> Having gifts that differ according to the grace given to us, let us use them: if prophecy, in proportion to our faith; if service, in our serving; he who teaches, in his teaching; he who exhorts, in his exhortation; he who contributes [gives money], in liberality; he who gives aid, with zeal; he who does acts of mercy, with cheerfulness. (Romans 12:3-8)

Paul wisely advised Christians to avoid both pride and false humility on account of their gifts. They must consider themselves with "sober judgment" and avoid selfish pride in their gifts and talents, while still *using* the gifts in faith for the good of others and the church. The purpose of the gifts is, once again, to serve Christ and the church, realizing how much Christians depend on each other's gifts for our human well-being and spiritual growth. Christians are not isolated individuals, but "individually members of one another." The use of spiritual gifts for the service of one another manifests and builds this unity in Christ. Paul urged Christians to be open to the spiritual gifts and to discern what is from God:

> Do not quench the Spirit, do not despise prophesying, but test everything; hold fast to what is good, abstain from every form of evil. (1 Thessalonians 5:19-22)

Much has been written in the Catholic Church in recent years about the discernment and proper use of all the gifts of the Spirit. In an audience with the Italian charismatic renewal in 1980, Pope John Paul II reaffirmed St. Paul's advice:

> I will say to you with St. Paul: "Test everything; hold fast what is good" (1 Thessalonians 5:21). Remain, therefore, in an attitude of constant and grateful availability for every gift that the Spirit wishes to pour into your hearts.[12]

Having said that charisms must be tested or discerned (a particular role of the pastors of the church), John Paul II proposed criteria for testing the validity of charisms and the presence of the Holy Spirit:

- Agreement with the church's faith in Jesus Christ (see 1 Corinthians 12:3);
- The presence of the fruit of the Spirit: love, joy, peace (see Galatians 5:22);

- Conformity with the church's authority and acceptance of its directives;
- Adherence to a simple rule for charisms used in the community: "Everything should be done for building up" (1 Corinthians 14:26).[13]

Pope Paul VI, addressing participants in an international Catholic charismatic renewal conference in Rome in 1975, advanced guidelines for discernment similar to those quoted above from Pope John Paul II. Paul VI claimed that the central principle for discerning the authenticity of spiritual gifts is the test of love. That is why in the First Letter to the Corinthians, St. Paul placed his great discourse on love (chapter thirteen) between an explanation of the charisms (chapter twelve) and a discussion of their practical use in the church (chapter fourteen). It is clear from reading 1 Corinthians 13 in this context that St. Paul is primarily teaching about using the gifts of the Holy Spirit in love, or else they are useless. As Pope Paul VI stated in his address,

> No matter how desirable spiritual goods are—and they are desirable—only the love of charity, agape, makes the Christian perfect; it alone makes people pleasing to God. This love not only presupposes a gift of the Spirit; it implies the active presence of his person in the heart of the Christian. . . .
>
> It is to love that are ordered all the gifts which the Spirit distributes to whom he wills, for it is love which builds up (see 1 Corinthians 8:1), just as it is love which, after Pentecost, made the first Christians into a community dedicated to fellowship (see Acts 2:42), everyone being "of one heart and soul" (Acts 4:32).[14]

It is tragic that charisms have been a source of contention in the church today, for they are God's gift to unify and build up his church. Further, the fact that *each* Christian has a charism for use in the church and the world is a source of the dignity of the Christian. There are no "ungifted" people, nor are there people who are meant to be entirely dependent on others. The unity of the church is built as we come to recognize each other's gifts and value them, instead of seeing ourselves as in competition with each other over who has the greater gift (or gifts). The gifts then lead to the glory and praise of God, who is their source, and who distributes them freely to all as he wills. The gifts of the Holy Spirit lead us to rely on God's grace in all things, and to the awareness that all our accomplishments are really his gifts. They also lead us to a greater awareness of the transcendent nature of the church as we yield to and foster the use of gifts such as prophecy, healing, discernment, and even speaking in tongues.

Let us follow the teaching of the Second Vatican Council and the *Catechism of the Catholic Church*, which urges us to accept the charisms—both those given to us and those given to others—with gratitude, as they make us "fit and ready to undertake various tasks and offices for the renewal and building up of the Church."[15]

CHAPTER EIGHT

The Spirit as Guarantee
of Our Inheritance

Imagine this conversation between an evangelical Christian and a Catholic:

Evangelical: "Have you been saved?"

Catholic: I'm not sure I understand your question. I'm a Catholic. I've been baptized, I go to church, and I try to keep the Ten Commandments."

Evangelical: "But, is Jesus Christ your Lord and Savior? Do you know that he has saved you from sin and death and that you will live forever with him in heaven?"

Catholic: "Yes, I know that Jesus died to save the human race from sin, and that he rose from the dead. As for heaven, well of course I hope that I will make it to heaven, and I think I'm on the right track. But it would be a bit presumptuous to say that I know I'm going to heaven."

Evangelical: "Well, then, if you don't know that—if you don't know whether you're saved—how can you call yourself a Christian?"

The Catholic in this dialogue responded in a typical fashion to a commonly asked question about salvation. However, if the Catholic respondent had known something more about the Holy Spirit and why he has been sent, the answer would have been even better. The Catholic would have known that the Holy Spirit had been given to us as an assurance of our final destiny in Christ.

Chapter four of this book discussed the powerful work of the Holy Spirit manifested in the fruits of the Spirit and the transformation of the moral life. One way that we can point to the saving work of Christ in our lives is by those works of the Holy Spirit within us.

The transforming work of God was so evident to the early Christians that St. Paul was able to say to the Christians in Corinth, based on his experience and theirs, that "if anyone is in Christ, he is a new creation; the old has passed away, behold, the new has come!" (2 Corinthians 5:17). Concerning God's law he said, "The written code kills, but the Spirit gives life" (2 Corinthians 3:6). Christians can know that Christ has saved them when they experience radical moral and spiritual transformation in their lives (the new creation) and when they see the works of the flesh being replaced, either gradually or with grace-filled rapidity, by the fruit of the Spirit.

However, St. Paul is even more explicit in his letters about the Holy Spirit's being a foretaste, or "first-fruit"—an actual beginning—of the life of resurrection. Christians believe that just as Christ has been raised from the dead, his faithful followers will be raised up with him after they die. St. Paul speaks at length about the firm and sure hope that Christians have in the resurrection of Jesus Christ and in their own future resurrection, which will be like Jesus' and will have been attained through his power (see 1 Corinthians 15).

St. Paul clearly indicated that the resurrection of Christians was to be a future event. He testified to his own experience of weakness and tribulations in this earthly life. Nonetheless, another important and surprising theme emerges in his writings: the Christian has a foretaste of the life of the resurrection in this life through his experience of the Holy Spirit.

For St. Paul, the Holy Spirit is more than the source of new life and moral transformation in this world. In addition, the experience of the Spirit is a sign, guarantee, down-payment, certification, and first-fruit of the life of the world to come, received by Christians as a gift from the risen Christ.

The Holy Spirit as a Guarantee or First Payment

Sometimes, as in the following passage, it is not obvious in St. Paul's writings what it is that the Spirit guarantees:

> For all the promises of God find their Yes in him. That is why we utter the Amen through him, to the glory of God. But it is God who establishes us with you in Christ, and has commissioned us; he has put his seal upon us and given his Spirit in our hearts as a guarantee [or "first payment"]. (2 Corinthians 1:20-22)

In other contexts, however, St. Paul makes clear that the promise of God that the Holy Spirit guarantees is the promise of the redemption of our bodies, or eternal life.

> For we know that if the earthly tent we live in is destroyed, we have a building from God, a house not made with hands, eternal in the heavens. Here indeed we groan and long to put on our heavenly dwelling, so that by putting it on we may not be found naked. For while we are still in this tent, we sigh with anxiety; not that we would be unclothed, but that we would be further clothed, so that what is mortal may be swallowed up by life. He who has prepared us for this very thing is God, who has given us the Spirit as a guarantee [first payment]. (2 Corinthians 5:1-5)

St. Paul is supremely confident in the reality of life beyond death. To him, the Holy Spirit is a guarantee of our reception of this eternal life. He is able to make this claim based upon the experience of the Christians he addressed. As one scholar, C. L. Mitton, puts it:

> In these five verses from 2 Corinthians 5, St. Paul makes special use of this undisputed fact of Christian experience. He appeals to it as something generally accepted and well-known in order to throw light on something less immediately familiar. The present possession of the Spirit St. Paul here calls "the earnest (guarantee) of the Spirit." This does not mean that God has already bestowed a small portion of the Spirit as a kind of token of a larger portion to come later. Rather, it is that the abundant outpouring of the Spirit, already known and appropriated, is an "earnest" here and now of the very life of heaven.[1]

The Greek word for "guarantee," or "earnest," is *arrabon*. To understand what St. Paul meant by these terms, it is helpful to determine the derivation and meaning of the Greek word, *arrabon*, from which they are translated. *Arrabon* was originally a legal term meaning something like a deposit: a partial payment guaranteeing that a full payment will be made at a later date.

Before the use of money was common in transactions, though, *arrabon* actually referred to a sample or foretaste of a product being purchased; this was given as a guarantee that the full amount of the purchase would be delivered on time and be of the same quality as the sample. The Spirit, then, is more than a legal guarantee of our eventual reception of our inheritance of eternal life, giving us some idea of its nature and quality.[2] The life in the Holy Spirit that we have on earth is really a foretaste, a sample of the life of heaven.

Do We "Experience" the Holy Spirit?

Can the possession of the Holy Spirit be spoken of as an experience? Realizing that this is a potential obstacle for understanding the Holy Spirit as a guarantee of eternal life, C. L. Mitton comments:

> Some may hesitate to speak of the experience of the Holy Spirit as something so real and personal, but we do well to remind ourselves that the absence of this experience was something which St. Paul could quickly detect in the group of Christians at Ephesus, and also he frequently speaks of this gift as "in our hearts" (e.g., 2 Corinthians. 1:22, Galatians. 4:6). It is a present reality of Christian experience.[3]

Mitton refers to the text of Acts 19:1-6, in which St. Paul abruptly asks a group of recently baptized followers of Christ, "Did you receive the Holy Spirit when you believed?" It was apparent to St. Paul that something essential to Christianity was missing from the lives of these converts—a "power shortage," as author Peter Kreeft speculated in a comment cited earlier. It is evident from their response to St. Paul's question that at the very least these converts had not been fully instructed in the Christian faith.

> And they said, "No, we have never even heard that there is a Holy Spirit." And he said, "Into what then were you baptized?" They said, "Into John's baptism." And Paul said, "John baptized with the baptism of repentance, telling the people to believe in the one who was to come after him, that is, Jesus." On hearing this, they were baptized in the name of the Lord Jesus. And when Paul had laid his hands upon

them, the Holy Spirit came on them; and they spoke in tongues and prophesied. (Acts 19:2-6)

But the problem with these converts in Ephesus was not just poor instruction. Because they had not received Christian baptism, they had no experience (as well as no idea) of the gift of the Holy Spirit and of how his coming was supposed to change their lives. The baptism they had undergone—John's baptism—was a sign of repentance and desire to turn away from sin and toward God. Christians begin to turn to God through this first, necessary step of repentance from sin; but, if this is all that happens, they are no better off than the disciples of John the Baptist in Jesus' time. One author writes,

The sect of John the Baptist was unaware that the Spirit existed, that the Messianic promises had been fulfilled and also that the Spirit was given in abundance. The sect practiced the eschatological baptism, ignoring the gift of the Holy Spirit.[4]

As we have seen, St. Paul was able to recognize the absence of the Spirit of God in the lives of those at Ephesus. They had come to believe in Jesus but had not yet been baptized. Would Christians today be able to testify from their own experience whether or not they had received the Holy Spirit? Unfortunately, I think many Christians would be uncertain. They would usually know that there is a Holy Spirit. But would they be able to affirm that the Holy Spirit was a God-given guarantee that they were to live forever? Could they articulate the fact that it is through the Holy Spirit they had experienced (or were experiencing) a foretaste of eternal life?

And yet, the experience of receiving the Spirit appears to be the best explanation of why St. Paul can speak with such deep-rooted assurance and conviction about the reality of the resurrection life. Indeed, beginning with his earliest writings, St. Paul associated the assurance of salvation and a glorified life with Christ with the Holy Spirit. He wrote to the Thessalonians,

> God chose you from the beginning to be saved through sanctification by the Spirit and belief in the truth. To this he called you through our gospel, so that you may obtain the glory of our Lord Jesus Christ. (2 Thessalonians 2:13-14)

"Glory" is one of St. Paul's many ways of describing the entry into this new mode of existence. His use of so many terms for it is not surprising, since the resurrection life is totally beyond both our experience and our imagination. Words can only capture glimpses of that existence. "Glory" expresses one of the more vivid aspects of resurrection life. As in the passage above, it designates the splendor and happiness we hope to obtain with Christ in the next life. Elsewhere, Paul refers to this hope as "an eternal weight of glory beyond all comparison" (2 Corinthians 4:17), promises that we shall be "raised in glory" (1 Corinthians 15:43), and insists that "the sufferings of this present time are not worth comparing with the glory that is to be revealed" (Romans 8:18).

Still Only a "Foretaste" of Heaven

Eternal life is a gift freely given to those who possess and live by the Holy Spirit. However, in spite of St. Paul's apparent assurance of the reception of this gift, which is guaranteed by the Christian's experience of the Spirit, he still realized that our salvation and redemption is ultimately a matter of hope. Though Christians may have confidence in the idea of eternal life, in the abstract, we also experience doubt, fear, and discouragement resulting from our sinfulness, our human nature, and our imperfect possession of the Spirit. St. Paul was careful not to mistake the experience of the Spirit in this life (as a "guarantee") for the full possession of the resurrection life itself. It is still only a foretaste of something that must be awaited with patience and faith. St. Paul makes this point clearly in his Letters to the Galatians and the Romans:

> For through the Spirit, by faith, we wait for the hope of righteousness. (Galatians 5:5)

> We ourselves, who have the first fruits of the Spirit, groan inwardly as we wait for adoption as sons, the redemption of our bodies. For in this hope we are saved. Now hope that is seen is not hope. For who hopes for what he sees? But if we hope for what we do not see, we wait for it with patience. (Romans 8:23-25)

The passage from Romans merits our special attention. Here Paul introduces a new metaphor to describe our possession of the Holy Spirit. The Spirit is *aparche*, meaning first-fruit, first installment, or down-payment. This Greek term is probably not merely a literary device but had an experiential referent in the early church. William Sanday, a nineteenth-century Scripture scholar, wrote that by *aparche*,

> St. Paul evidently means all the phenomena of that great outpouring which was especially characteristic of the apostolic age from the day of Pentecost onward, the varied *charismata* bestowed upon the first Christians (1 Corinthians 12, etc.), but including also the moral and spiritual gifts which were more perma-

nent (Galatians 5:22f). The possession of these gifts serve to quicken the sense of the yet greater gifts that were to come.[5]

Most commentators today would agree with Sanday and see a virtual identity in the meanings of *arrabon* and *aparche* in St. Paul's thought. But C. Clark Oke has found a different shade of meaning in *aparche,* based on his analysis of its context in Romans. He claims that *aparche* is a more active term than *arrabon*—that it implies that the Holy Spirit is an active principle, more active even than "first-fruit" would indicate—and that it refers specifically to the *status* of the believer. His conclusion is that *aparche* is better understood as a birth certificate or certification: this, he says, better conveys the sense of activity and the new status given to the believer by the Spirit.[6]

In any case, *aparche* unquestionably indicates both the believers' experiential awareness of the Holy Spirit and the incompleteness of their possession of what has been pledged as first-fruit, first installment, down-payment, or birth certificate, in the form of the Spirit. We possess the Spirit, but we still groan along with all creation, as we await the redemption of our bodies (see Romans 8:22-23). Human existence is still troubled and limited, and so we must continue to live in hope. J. D. G. Dunn notes that St. Paul avoided the view of the Gnostics (an early heretical group) that the full Christian experience could be "achieved here and now." Rather, Dunn argues, Paul

recognizes that the full flowering of the life of Christ in him involves the experience of death as well as of life; he shares Christ's risen life through the Spirit, but not fully; there is still a futureness in Christian experience, a "not yet"; he is in the process of being transformed into the image of Christ, but he does not yet fully bear that image; the Spirit is only the *arrabon* and *aparche* of a life fully vivified and determined by the Spirit. . . . Otherwise "hope" would be a meaningless concept.[7]

St. Paul's characterization of the Spirit as a "guarantee" is a model of balance between bold optimism and cautious realism. The Spirit is unmistakably portrayed as the sure hope of our attainment of eternal life, and yet hope must remain hope. Its object cannot be realized in this life. Our hope in the Spirit is again inseparably connected with the role of Jesus. The Spirit witnesses to Jesus because the fundamental reason for our hope is Jesus' resurrection: "If Christ has not been raised, then our preaching is in vain" (1 Corinthians 15:14).

But just as sin came into the world through one man (Adam), and through sin death (see Romans 5:12), the "last Adam" (Jesus Christ) overcame sin by his death, "that grace also might reign through righteousness to eternal life through Jesus Christ our Lord" (Romans 5:21). St. Paul masterfully brought together and blended these themes of Christ's work, our hope in his glory, our gradual transformation into his image in this life, and the manifestation of the Spirit as our guarantee of the fulfillment of this hope:

> Therefore, since we are justified by faith, we have peace with God through our Lord Jesus Christ. Through him we have obtained access to this grace in which we stand, and we rejoice in our hope of sharing the glory of God. More than that, we rejoice in our sufferings, knowing that suffering produces endurance, and endurance produces character, and character produces hope, and hope does not disappoint us,

because God's love has been poured into our hearts through the Holy Spirit which has been given to us. (Romans 5:1-5)

The Holy Spirit is thus manifested in power and love, so that Christians may persevere in hope and faith in this life. They are not driven to despair by suffering, nor do they cease rejoicing when trouble comes. Rather, the Holy Spirit makes even suffering a source of hope and an occasion to turn more fully to God. St. Paul's benediction at the end of the letter to the Romans is quite apropos: "May the God of hope fill you with all joy and peace in believing, so that by the power of the Holy Spirit you may abound in hope" (Romans 15:13). The Spirit is indeed the inward guarantee that the promises of God will be fulfilled!

The Seal of the Spirit

If we are baptized, we belong to God in Jesus Christ and we have received the gift of the Holy Spirit, who is the guarantee of our eternal inheritance. In the New Testament letters, baptism is also referred to as a "seal" or "sealing" with the Holy Spirit. As we see in the Scripture texts below, the seal of the Spirit received in baptism is related to the idea that the Holy Spirit is the guarantee of our eternal inheritance:

But it is God who establishes us with you in Christ, and has commissioned us; he has put his seal upon us and given us his Spirit in our hearts as a guarantee. (2 Corinthians 1:21-22)

In him you also, who have heard the word of truth, the gospel of your salvation, and have believed in

him, were sealed with the promised Holy Spirit, who is the guarantee of our inheritance until we acquire possession of it, to the praise of his glory.
(Ephesians 1:13-14)

And do not grieve the Holy Spirit of God, in whom you were sealed for the day of redemption.
(Ephesians 4:30)

Scholars are in almost unanimous agreement that this notion of "sealing" is a reference to baptism. The noted Catholic biblical scholar Rudolph Schnackenburg thinks that "seal" and "guarantee" are complementary ideas about the Holy Spirit: he sees "seal" as the sense of baptism as an outward stamp or sign, and "guarantee" as a term stressing the way we experience the Spirit within.[8]

Both "seal" and "guarantee" express the manifestation of the Spirit, but express different aspects of the reality: the outward sign of baptism, which is visible to all, and the internal, experiential mode known only to the believer. Both aspects of the Spirit's manifestation are apparently part of St. Paul's thought.

In our own time, Christians commonly accept the idea that baptism is an outward sign of the believer's receiving the Spirit and belonging to God and his church. But the aspect of "guarantee"—the inward, experiential work of the Spirit in the baptized person as an assurance of belonging to God and being granted the gift of salvation—is often neglected or forgotten. Clearly, when a person is baptized as an infant, he or she is not able to comprehend the immediate experience of receiving the Spirit as a guarantee of salvation. But, in the early church of St. Paul's day, people were baptized as adults and commonly received the Holy Spirit and his gifts in power. As scholar A. M. Hunter explains,

> The linkage of baptism with the Spirit is surely pre-Pauline and primitive. . . . Normally . . . the reception of the Spirit must have synchronized with the act of baptism. Baptism must have been for the convert a moment of new power when, with solemn ceremony, he turned his back on the old life and began the new. . . . He possibly prophesied or spoke with tongues—he felt an inrush of the Holy Spirit. Moreover, by baptism he became a member of the holy community—the sphere in which the Holy Spirit moved and wrought.[9]

Hunter goes on to state that the connection of baptism with the reception of the Spirit was probably not a doctrine peculiar to St. Paul, "but an experience felt, in varying degree, by every convert for the first days of the Christian church."[10]

Does that mean that people baptized as infants can't receive the Holy Spirit as the inward guarantee of both the Christian's new identity in Jesus Christ and Christ's gift of eternal life? No. The fact is that adult Christians are supposed to have some "experiential" knowledge of the Holy Spirit, even to the extent that was known in the primitive church. As we have seen, St. Paul understands the experience of the Spirit as an important and normal aspect of the Christian life. Now that God is renewing the church in the Holy Spirit, Catholics and other Christians are discovering that the Holy Spirit is more than just a theological concept or a person of God to be accepted purely on faith with no basis in human experience. The Holy Spirit is being experienced by hundreds of thousands of baptized Christians as a living person who is a guarantee of acceptance by God and a pledge, first-fruit, and foretaste of eternal life with God in heaven. People who have experienced this renewal of the grace of the Holy Spirit ("renewal" because the Spirit is initially received in baptism and dwells within a person from that point on) know that God is real, that he loves them, and that he is leading them in Christ to eternal life.

Again, it must be said that this experience of the Spirit can be explained away, minimized, denied, and rejected—even by those who have been touched by God with this special grace. It does remain a matter of *faith* that it *is* the Holy Spirit who has touched a person's life and that this experience truly is a God-given guarantee or pledge of salvation. Experiences may be interpreted in many ways, and doubts may enter even about whether anything has happened at all.

However, sacred Scripture and Christian experience testify that, both in the early church and today, the Holy Spirit has been lavished upon God's people as a source of hope and assurance that all God's promises, especially the promise of eternal life, will be fulfilled. As the first-fruit of this eternal life, the Holy Spirit enables the Christian to experience (albeit in a partial, veiled way) the life of heaven, even here on earth, through the gifts and fruits of the Spirit manifested in our lives. I have heard a saying that even on earth, the way to hell is already "hell," and the way to heaven is "heavenly." The Holy Spirit gives Christians a share in the joy of heaven, even now.

Recalling our dialogue at the beginning of the chapter, how could our Catholic have responded to the question, "Have you been saved?" Perhaps the simplest answer would be, "Yes, I have been saved by Jesus Christ, and I hope to persevere in following Jesus and in accepting his gift of salvation until the end of my life." And I would hope that after reading this chapter, our Catholic respondent might also say, "I already have experienced the gift of salvation through the Holy Spirit whom God has given me. If I continue to live in the Holy Spirit and follow his guidance, I trust that I will receive the fullness of salvation that Jesus has promised his people!"

CHAPTER NINE

Unity: The Spirit's Greatest Gift

Tension, discord, and division seem to be hallmarks of human relationships. We have come to expect (and, sadly, to accept) these conditions in world affairs and in our countries and communities. Tragically, division also mars relationships among Christians. The fact that Christians are divided into hundreds, if not thousands, of separated church groups and denominations stands in stark opposition to Jesus' last "high-priestly" prayer for his followers: "that they may all be one even as thou, Father, art in me, and I in thee . . . that they may be one even as we are one . . . so that the world may know that thou hast sent me . . ." (John 17:21-23). Even within the Catholic Church, people are polarized and divided into groups, which causes confusion and, sometimes, scandal.

In the Beginning . . .

How did this tragic situation of discord come about? We learn from Scripture that God's intention when he created us was that we live in unity grounded in truth and love. The counter-purpose of Satan was to create division and disunity flowing from lies, deception, and hatred.

From the beginning of the book of Genesis, we see that God originally brought forth his creation in perfect harmony. Man and woman, the crown of material creation, were created in perfect harmony and intimacy with God, their Creator, and with each other. However, disunity did exist in the realm of the purely spiritual beings. Satan, or Lucifer, a great archangel, had freely chosen to divide himself from God and his love, and he brought other angels with him. After his rebellion, Satan also sought to destroy the unity of the first humans with God and with each other. And we know that he succeeded.

The deception and lies of Satan effectively destroyed the unity God had created. Adam and Eve sought to lay the blame for their disobedience on someone else: the man, on the woman; and the woman, on the serpent. The first-born of Adam and Eve, Cain, proceeded to kill his younger brother out of jealousy. Then, he tried to deny his guilt and his responsibility. ("Am I my brother's keeper?"—Genesis 4:9). Genesis reports that the wickedness and corruption of humanity grew so great that eventually God destroyed the whole human race, saving only Noah and his family. When people multiplied again through the offspring of Noah, they shared a common language and sought to build a great city, Babel, and "a tower with its top in the heavens." Through this project they wanted to "make a name" for themselves— a sin of pride that resulted in disunity: God punished them by confusing their language so that they could not understand one another. And so they were dispersed, scattered over the face of the earth (see Genesis 11:1-9).

Biblical scholars may argue over the historicity of these accounts, but there is one indisputable truth that we see in Genesis and in all the Hebrew Scriptures: from the beginning, rebellion against God has resulted in increasing hatred and disunity. Throughout human history, the cancer of disunity has expressed itself in everything from massive wars to petty daily hatreds and divisions among neighbors and within families. Satan's motto may well be "divide and conquer," for he knows that a people united in faith and in God's love cannot be vanquished, but a people divided become easy prey for his lies and deceptions. Accepting Satan's lies leads to separation from God, which, ultimately, is eternal death.

The Holy Spirit: Our Hope for Unity

What hope, then, does the human race have for unity? If we look at the history of the centuries following the coming of Jesus Christ, it doesn't appear that things have changed substantially from the days of Genesis. Have not Christians been equally responsible for great wars and prone to the same petty divisions and hatreds in daily life as their forebears in faith of pre-Christian Judaism?

And yet, if we believe sacred Scripture, then we must accept that there was a time when unity was not just a dream or a wild hope, but a reality. Further, Scripture reveals that God has actually given his church the "secret" to unity.

This unity that the world seeks was manifested at Pentecost. Jews who were dispersed all over the Roman world (reminding us of the scattering of the people after Babel was destroyed) had come together at Jerusalem to celebrate the Jewish feast of Weeks, or Pentecost. These Jews from different countries were in the crowd when Peter burst forth from the upper room and addressed them; miraculously, all these Jews, with their various languages, clearly understood what Peter was saying, and they were "amazed and perplexed" at this (Acts 2:5-13). *The confusion of languages at Babel was reversed by the unity of speech at Pentecost!*

When some mocking skeptics refused to believe the miracle and attributed it to drunkenness, Peter directly refuted their claim. He announced that they were witnessing the fulfillment of Joel's prophecy—accompanied by clear signs to demonstrate it—that in the last days, God would pour out his Spirit upon all flesh (see Acts 2:14-21).

In the days that followed Pentecost, the signs continued. Healings and miracles were performed through the apostles in the name of Jesus. The greatest sign, though, was the love and unity of the followers of Christ. Had not Jesus taught, "By this all men will know that you are my disciples, if you have love for one another" (John 13:35)? This love and unity was apparent in the life of the first community of Christians in Jerusalem:

> And fear came upon every soul; and many wonders and signs were done through the apostles. And all who believed were together and had all things in common; and they sold their possessions and goods and distributed them to all, as any had need.
>
> And day by day, attending the temple together and breaking bread in their homes, they partook of food with glad and generous hearts, praising God and having favor with all the people. And the Lord added to their number day by day those who were being saved. (Acts 2:43-47)

Acts of the Apostles: A False Picture of Unity?

As we saw in chapter two, some scholars say that the Acts of the Apostles presents an idealized, unreal picture of the first Christian community. If this were so, why would the author proceed to talk about the shocking deaths of Ananias and Sapphira (see Acts 5), the dispute over the distribution of food to widows (see Acts 6), and the great controversy over whether gentile converts to Christ needed to be circumcised, culminating in the first great council of elders of the church in Jerusalem (see Acts 15)?

If St. Luke set out to paint an idyllic picture of Christian unity and love in the Acts of the Apostles, he certainly did a poor job of it. The truth is that the first Christians in Jerusalem were truly united in heart and mind, and so they were respected, and their numbers grew rapidly. That controversies and disputes did arise is not surprising. What is remarkable (as Acts reports) is that God intervened to resolve the difficulties.

This intervention was not usually as dramatic as were the deaths of Ananias and Sapphira after they had "tempted," or lied to, the Spirit of God. Normally, the people of the young church experienced God's presence when they turned to him for help to resolve difficulties. It was the Holy Spirit who provided the wisdom and guidance that healed divisions and restored unity and peace among believers. Thus, we learn from the Acts of the Apostles that true unity is *possible* and that it is a *gift* of the Holy Spirit. Nevertheless, unity is not something static to be taken for granted: it must be sought constantly by listening to the Holy Spirit and being filled and renewed with his love again and again.

Unity is a task as much as it is a gift; or, rather, it is a task accomplished only by means of a gift—the gift of the Holy Spirit. The Holy Spirit is given to bring about unity in the church, based on love, and yet the church and its members still battle with sinfulness, with the allurements of the world, and with Satan—all of which can undermine or even destroy God's gift of unity. That is why the Scriptures repeatedly exhort the followers of Christ to be "eager to maintain the unity of the Spirit in the bond of peace" (Ephesians 4:3).

The Charisms and Unity

Of all the churches that St. Paul addressed in his letters, the church in Corinth was probably the most "Spirit-filled," or "charismatic." Paul commented that this local church was "not lacking in any spiritual gift" (1 Corinthians 1:7). And yet, the community was beset with difficulties. St. Paul received word of problems in Corinth and wrote,

It has been reported to me by Chloe's people that there is quarreling among you, my brethren. What I mean is that each one of you says, "I belong to Paul," or "I belong to Apollos," or "I belong to Cephas," or "I belong to Christ." Is Christ divided? (1 Corinthians 1:11-13)

As the letter proceeds, the depth of the difficulties of the church in Corinth is more fully revealed. Grievances between members of the church were apparently being settled in secular courts, with Christians bringing lawsuits against Christians (see 1 Corinthians 6:1-8). Some Christians were scandalizing others by eating food that had been used in pagan rituals (see 1 Corinthians 8). Worse, Paul heard that when the community gathered to eat the Lord's Supper, which at the time included an *agape* meal, "one is hungry and another is drunk" (1 Corinthians 11:21). Also, Paul thought it necessary to devote an extensive section of his letter to correcting misunderstandings and abuses regarding the use of the gifts of the Holy Spirit (see 1 Corinthians 12-14).

If we look closely at St. Paul's counsel to the church in Corinth, we will discover that he identifies the most important sign of the Holy Spirit's presence in a Christian body. In the spirit of 1 Corinthian 13, here is how I would describe Paul's "test" of whether the Holy Spirit is present in fullness in a particular group or community.

If I were to visit a Christian group that was vibrant in worship, that manifested a wide variety of gifts of the Holy Spirit, and showing profound reverence, I would be impressed and grateful, but I would not be certain that the Holy Spirit fully ruled that group.

And if this Christian group not only worshiped vibrantly and reverently but also had a deeply committed ministry to the needy and poor or to evangelization or to visiting the sick and imprisoned, I would heartily rejoice, but I would not yet know whether that group was fully yielded to the Holy Spirit.

Finally, if someone were to ask me, "What, then, *is* the surest, most reliable sign of the presence of the Holy Spirit?" I would respond without hesitation, "Unity—that is, a deep authentic unity based on God's truth and, most of all, on God's love."

Now, one could argue that no group or community of Christians is ever, or has ever been, perfect in their holiness or in their abandonment to the grace and guidance of the Holy Spirit. However, what if I visited a group and found— regardless of their prayer life or their apostolate—that the members consistently loved and served each other? What if I found that they really worked out divisive differences and disagreements, always forgave each other, and were deeply *united* to each other in the love of Christ? What if their trust and unity was such that they left each other free to be truly themselves, and even to hold diverse opinions about matters not essential to faith or to common life? Then I would be certain that the Holy Spirit governed that group! I would also be fairly confident that their prayer and their apostolate were tremendously rich and fruitful, with their prayer as the *source,* and their apostolate as the *expression* of their loving unity through the grace of the Holy Spirit.

United in the Lordship of Christ

Unity is a gift of the Holy Spirit, and Christians are united in professing and living the fact that Jesus is Lord of the community. Only the Holy Spirit can enable the community to recognize and profess with one voice that Jesus is truly Lord of them all (1 Corinthians 12:3).

If Jesus is Lord, then there can be no factions or divisions in the church. No one can say "I'm for Paul" or "I'm for Apollos." It was Jesus Christ who was crucified for us, and by the one Spirit that Jesus poured out, "we were all baptized into one body—Jews or Greeks, slaves or free—and all made to drink of one Spirit" (1 Corinthians 12:13). The result is that Christians, as members of Christ's body, literally belong to each other, are "individually members one of another" (Romans 12:5; 1 Corinthians 12:27), just as the parts of a human body belong to each other and must function together to survive.

This theme of the unity of believers in Jesus Christ and through the Holy Spirit is emphasized often in the Pauline writings. In the Letter to the Galatians, Paul urges,

> If we live by the Spirit, let us also walk by the Spirit. Let us have no self-conceit, no provoking of one another, no envy of one another. . . . As we have opportunity, let us do good to all men, and especially to those who are of the household of faith. (Galatians 5:25-26; 6:10)

The Letter to the Colossians speaks of Jesus as the source and the goal of the unity of the whole cosmos:

> He is before all things, and in him all things hold together. He is the head of the body, the church; he is the beginning, the first-born from the dead, that in everything he might be preeminent. For in him all the fullness of God was pleased to dwell, and through him to reconcile to himself all things, whether on earth or in heaven, making peace by the blood of his cross. (Colossians 1:17-20)

Similar themes are to be found in the Letter to the Ephesians. There, we read that Christ is our peace, that he has reconciled divided humanity and brought us together in the unity of the church, with "Christ Jesus himself being the cornerstone, in whom the whole structure is joined together and grows into a holy temple in the Lord; in whom you also are built into it for a dwelling place of God in the Spirit" (Ephesians 2:20-22). Because of what Christ has done for us, Ephesians exhorts us to

lead a life worthy of the calling to which you have been called, with all lowliness and meekness, with patience, forbearing one another in love, eager to maintain the unity of the Spirit in the bond of peace. There is one body and one Spirit, just as you were called to the one hope that belongs to your call, one Lord, one faith, one baptism, one God and Father of us all who is above all and through all and in all. (Ephesians 4:1-6)

Christians are not to be divided. "Rather, speaking the truth in love, we are to grow up in every way into him who is the head, into Christ, from whom the whole body . . . when each part is working properly, makes bodily growth and upbuilds itself in love" (Ephesians 4:15-16).

As in Colossians, the Letter to the Ephesians continues with a powerful section urging Christians to denounce falsehood, anger, stealing, evil talk, and other vices. It urges Christians to say only things that edify others: "Be kind to one another, tenderhearted, forgiving one another, as God in Christ forgave you" (Ephesians 4:32). To preserve unity, Christians are to "be subject to one another out of reverence for Christ" (Ephesians 5:21).

Similar themes appear in St. Paul's Letter to the Philippians. He urges the community,

Only let your manner of life be worthy of the gospel of Christ, so that whether I come and see you or am absent, I may hear of you that you stand firm in one spirit, with one mind striving side by side for the faith of the gospel. . . .

So if there is any encouragement in Christ, any incentive of love, any participation in the Spirit, any affection and sympathy, complete my joy by being of the same mind, having the same love, being in full accord and of one mind. Do nothing from self-ishness or conceit, but in humility count others better than yourselves. Let each of you look not only to his own interests, but also to the interests of others. (Philippians 1:27; 2:1-4)

St. Paul frequently returns to this theme of Christian unity in Jesus Christ through the Holy Spirit. This unity is surely a clear sign of the reign or lordship of Christ, which can only be established by the Holy Spirit's power. St. John's gospel reveals that the model of this unity is the blessed Trinity, God himself. As we saw at the beginning of the chapter, Jesus prayed earnestly at the Last Supper that his followers would experience this perfect unity, too:

I do not pray for these only, but also for those who believe in me through their word, that they may all be one; even as thou, Father, art in me, and I in thee, that they also may be in us, so that the world may believe that thou hast sent me. The glory which thou hast given me I have given to them, that they may be one even as we are one, I in them and thou in me, that they may become perfectly one, so that the world may know that thou hast sent me and hast loved them even as thou hast loved me. (John 17:20-23)

Unity in Christian Life

Another sign of the Holy Spirit's presence or absence in a community is the behavior, or conduct, of its members in their daily lives. The community doesn't have to be perfect or sinless—that will happen only when the Lord himself comes again to judge and purify the earth! Nevertheless, the fruit of the Holy Spirit must be evident in the lives of the members of the community.

The purpose of the Holy Spirit's presence in the believer and in the Christian community is to bring forth good fruit in daily life and conduct. According to St. Paul, where the "works of the flesh" (Galatians 5:19-21) are present, there is dissension and division. Where the "fruit of the Spirit"—consisting of love, joy, peace, patience, kindness, generosity, faithfulness, gentleness, self-control (Galatians 5:22-23)—is manifest, there is unity and peace.

Pope John Paul II explained the relationship between these gifts of the spirit and unity in his general audience of January 20, 1993:

The adoption of these interior dispositions, conforming the believer ever more closely to Christ, impels him towards an ever deeper communion with his brothers and sisters. Christ is indeed one, as is the Spirit who is the source of these interior dispositions. Therefore gifts, charisms and virtues—when they are authentic—*tend concordantly and harmoniously toward unity.* In presenting this broad list of virtues, the apostle significantly calls each of them "*the* fruit—*ho karpos*—of the Spirit": the various virtues, in their diversity, come together in the "one fruit" of the Spirit, which is love. St. Paul explains this to the first Christians of Rome: "The love of God has been poured out into our hearts through the Holy Spirit that has been given to us" (Romans 5:5). The love of God (*agape*) is shown by self-control and gentleness, in understanding for one's neighbor, in cordial relations in a willingness to forgive. . . . These are the essential prerequisites for truly seeking unity.[1]

It is notable that both the fruit and the gifts of the Holy Spirit are involved in the promotion of the church's unity. As we discussed in chapter seven, St. Paul speaks of using the gifts of the Spirit (charisms) for the "building up" of the church (see 1 Corinthians 3:10), or for the "common good."

Günther Bornkamm, an expert on the theology of St. Paul, comments that Paul's "guiding principle" was responsibility toward others.[2] St. Paul clearly taught that every member of the church had a duty to edify the rest, following the example of Christ. For instance, Paul's entire argument concerning the use of the gifts of tongues and prophecy in 1 Corinthians 14 rested on this understanding of the responsibility of each believer to build up the church in an enlightened manner. For Paul, the Spirit was at work to draw men and women together in Christ, and only when the Spirit was present, was unity possible. Baptism was the paradigm for the unity that God intended. "For by one Spirit we were all baptized into one body—Jews or Greeks, slaves or free—and all were made to drink of one Spirit" (Corinthians 12:13).

The Centrality of Love

In the midst of his discussion of the proper use of the spiritual gifts for building up the church, St. Paul inserted his poetic and powerful chapter on the greatest sign of the Holy Spirit's presence:

Love is patient and kind; love is not jealous or boastful; it is not arrogant or rude. Love does not insist on its own way; it is not irritable or resentful; it does not rejoice at wrong, but rejoices in the right. Love bears all things, believes all things, hopes all things, endures all things.

Love never ends; as for prophecies, they will pass away; as for tongues, they will cease; as for knowledge, it will pass away. For our knowledge is imperfect and our prophecy is imperfect; but when the perfect comes, the imperfect will pass away. (1 Corinthians 13:4-10)

Pope John Paul II has also stressed the centrality of love in the Holy Spirit's action of bringing about unity:

Experience has amply shown that the relations between believers and communities seeking full communion *must be grounded in mutual love* based on the new commandment given by Jesus Christ to his disciples: "Love one another as I have loved you" (John 13:34).

It is in the context of mutual love, a reflection of God's love for us, that we can understand others and recognize their right intentions, even when their convictions are different. Without true love, mental reservations, mistrust and mutual suspicion occur and take hold. They can even lead to attributing intentions to one's neighbor that he does not have.

This is the reason why we strive to promote the so-called *"dialogue of charity"* as the normal context of ecumenical relations. It should be further deepened by removing the causes that can impede or diminish it.

Genuine love highlights fidelity to the Lord's will and thus prepares the heart to accept the truth in its entirety.[3]

God has called the church to be a people of love, a people whose conduct reflects the image of God himself.

The Challenge of Christian Unity

Earlier in this chapter, I claimed that a community could be blessed with a full range of spiritual gifts for worship and even called to extraordinary ministries of service (such as to the poor, or to evangelization), but still not be fully governed by the Holy Spirit.

Such a situation may sound implausible—but is it? The early church in Corinth seems to have had this problem. It had a superabundance of spiritual gifts, and yet, the divisions in the community, its misuse of the gifts, and all the other problems St. Paul addressed were signs that the community lacked love.

In our time, we find numerous examples of Christian groups with extraordinary ministries of evangelization, service to the poor, or other notable outreaches that have ended up plagued by scandal or division. Even where actual division has been avoided by the grace of the Holy Spirit, many churches or groups within churches continue to live with difficult internal divisions, tensions, parties, and factions. Often they accept this situation as unavoidable, or even normal.

The fact is that unity—true unity of mind and heart produced by the Holy Spirit as a fruit of love—is extremely difficult for any group of people to achieve and maintain, even within the church. And even when such unity is attained, it is constantly threatened and challenged; and so, it must be nurtured and guarded with vigilance and prayer.

The most visible sign of disunity in the church is Christianity's division into thousands of separate (and sometimes hostile) groups or "denominations." The New Testament witnesses how earnestly the leaders of the primitive church sought to avoid such divisions and how frequently they sought to resolve differences and preserve unity through the action of the Holy Spirit (see Acts 6 and 15). The early Christians embraced the teaching of Jesus that "all men will know that you are my disciples, if you have love for one another" (John 13:35). They tried hard to maintain the unity for which Jesus had offered his "high priestly" prayer (see John 17:23).

The Decree on Ecumenism of the Second Vatican Council says that the division of Christians "openly contradicts the will of Christ and harms that most holy cause, the preaching of the gospel to every creature." And yet, where sin has abounded, God is supplying his superabundant grace so that his church will not fail. In the twentieth century, which might be called the "century of the Holy Spirit," God has stirred up among Christians a movement of grace seeking to restore the unity of the church. The same section of the Decree on Ecumenism goes on to speak of this hopeful development:

> Everywhere large numbers have felt the impulse of this grace, and among our separated brethren there also increases from day to day a movement, fostered by the grace of the Holy Spirit, for the restoration of unity among all Christians.[4]

It is not surprising that this ecumenical movement began in the twentieth century among Protestant missionaries who realized that the division and competition among their groups in the mission lands was a scandal and was hindering "that most holy cause, the preaching of the gospel to every creature."

What better chance the world would have of believing in Jesus Christ and his gospel if Christians were one, united by the Holy Spirit in truth and in love! Not only is this God's heartfelt desire, revealed by Jesus himself, but it is a necessity if the truth of the gospel is to shine forth in all its power and beauty.

The True Goal of Ecumenism

Many Christians think that the ultimate goal of the ecumenical movement—full unity of all the followers of Christ in the one, holy, catholic, and apostolic church that Jesus founded—is wishful thinking, a dream . . . impossible. Many Christians see this as so futile that they will not even *attempt* to be ecumenical, to promote Christian unity, even in their own attitudes and thoughts. Others fear a false ecumenism that sacrifices truth for the sake of unity.

It is easy to comfort ourselves with the thought that we still can be saved in our own church, and that our own church is at least as good as, if not superior to, other Christian churches or groups. We can try to convince ourselves that other Christians are not interested in unity, and that most don't even know what "ecumenism" means. Actually, it *is* uncomfortable and difficult to try to understand people with different religious beliefs and to try to explain our own. And anyway, why bother people with something they probably aren't interested in anyway?

These excuses are all silenced by Jesus' prayer for unity. We know that it is God's desire that there be only "one flock, one shepherd" (John 10:16). We are discouraged, because we see the impossibility of achieving Christian unity by our own efforts. It is evident that achieving unity is impossible by human effort or good will alone. It is also clear to those who have worked in the movement for Christian unity that our own plans about how unity can or will be achieved are sorely insufficient. Certain things are essential: increasing prayer for unity, honest effort to listen and seek to understand others and to present our own position as clearly as possible, and most importantly, the willingness and deep desire to forgive and to be forgiven for past wrongs and hurts—real or imagined.

Unity is ultimately a gift of God—and particularly a work of the Holy Spirit, who is the Spirit of truth and of love. The attitude of the Catholic Church toward Christian unity is summarized beautifully by the final paragraph of the Decree on Ecumenism:

> This most sacred Synod urgently desires that the initiatives of the sons of the Catholic Church, joined with those of the separated brethren, go forward without obstructing the ways of divine Providence and without prejudging the future inspiration of the Holy Spirit. Further, this Synod declares its realization that the holy task of reconciling all Christians in the unity of the one and only Church of Christ transcends human energies and abilities. It therefore places its hope entirely in the prayer of Christ for the Church, in the love of the Father for us, and in the power of the Holy Spirit. "And hope does not disappoint, because the charity of God is poured forth in our hearts by the Holy Spirit who has been given to us" (Romans. 5:5).[5]

The Catholic Tradition of Unity

Unity, that precious gift of the Holy Spirit, must be sought on the worldwide level through the ecumenical movement. The Catholic Church has a unique contribution to offer to this movement because of its heritage of preserving unity in spite of its vast geographic range; its experience of generations and even centuries of radical political and social change and upheavals; dozens of distinct varieties of Catholic spirituality and theology; and tremendous diversity in culture, language, and racial and ethnic backgrounds among its more than a billion members—about one-sixth of the world's population. In spite of all this, the Catholic Church has preserved the precious gift of visible unity for nearly two thousand years, far longer than the greatest nations and empires that have existed on earth!

For Catholics, therefore, unity is both a special gift of God to the church and a goal to be constantly worked toward through love. Among all the Christian churches and ecclesial communities, the Catholic Church bears a special tradition of unity. However, for the Catholic Church as a whole, as well as for any of the groups within it, unity also is a gift that is constantly threatened and can only be maintained with vigilance and prayer.

Obstacles to Christian Unity

Although unity has been a particular charism of the Catholic Church over the ages, we recognize that there is significant disunity even within our own church. One of the reasons disagreements arise among individual Christians and within Christian groups is simply that living the full Christian life consistently—always following the guidance of the Holy Spirit and in the Spirit's way of love—is difficult. At best, the life of a Christian or Christian group has peaks and valleys—times of fervor and great fidelity to the Lord, and times of dryness, struggle, failure, and even radical sin and infidelity. This is true of the history of the church as a whole, as well as of the individual groups within the church.

By the special grace of God, Jesus and Mary lived so completely by the grace and guidance of the Holy Spirit that they never fell into sin. And yet, even they experienced dryness, struggle, and perhaps even a sense of failure.

Many of the people whom the church recognizes as the greatest saints and model Christians were also, at some point, in great need of forgiveness and reconciliation. Among those who began as great sinners or weak followers of Christ but ended as great saints were St. Peter, St. Thomas, St. Paul, and St. Augustine, to name a few.

Likewise, some Christian groups that have been notable models of Christian witness have at certain times fallen into serious sin or error. We see this, for example, in the Bible's description of the seven churches in the Book of Revelation. In church history there are numerous examples of Christian groups, movements, or religious communities that illustrate this tendency.

How do we view and deal with individuals or Christian groups that are experiencing problems or struggles? The church in Galatia in St. Paul's day is one example of a community that had slipped into error and needed to be corrected and then reconciled with a broader church. The apostle had strong words for these Christians who, after "beginning in the Spirit," now risked "ending in the flesh."

> O foolish Galatians! Who has bewitched you, before whose eyes Jesus Christ was publicly portrayed as crucified? Let me ask you only this: Did you receive the Spirit by works of the law or by hearing with faith? Are you so foolish? Having begun with the Spirit, are you now ending with the flesh? Did you experience so many things in vain? (Galatians 3:1-4)

Does the Galatians' slip into sinfulness mean that the Holy Spirit was never with them, or that somewhere along the way, he abandoned them? No, it simply bears witness to the fact that consistently following the guidance of the Holy Spirit is very difficult. Learning to love and to work through differences, to forgive wrongs and to start over in relationships, to admit errors—especially errors arising from excess or misdirected zeal and fervor for Christ—all of these are necessary for the Christian, but all are exceedingly challenging!

One aspect of the canonization process in the Catholic Church acknowledges just how challenging it is to live in unity. In determining whether the person in question is a saint, the church looks for solid evidence of miracles worked through that person's intercession. The successful founding of a religious order or community in the church is counted as equivalent to just such a miracle. Indeed, given the challenges to unity and holiness, founding a successful Christian community or order is a miracle in every sense of the word!

Sometimes, when such groups experience severe difficulty or struggle, it could be a sign that the Holy Spirit does not wish the group to continue. Normally, though, it appears that the Holy Spirit's plan for such groups is not destruction but healing, reconciliation, and renewal. St. Paul had strong words of guidance and correction for the churches in Galatia and Corinth, but he did not abandon them or ask them to disband. The same is true of the author of the Book of Revelation, writing to the seven churches in Asia.

When Unity Is Threatened

So, what should a group within the Catholic Church—such as a parish, a religious order, or a lay community—do, when it experiences turmoil that threatens its unity? The first important step is for the group to recognize what is happening. It takes real insight, honesty, and spiritual sensitivity to see—through the grace and love of the Holy Spirit—that there is a problem.

As with any disease, the sooner the disease of disunity is discovered, the greater the likelihood that it can be healed. Sometimes the symptoms of disunity are very subtle, especially if the group values unity and if views or feelings that may divide the group are either subtly or consciously suppressed. For example, it is possible to confuse external conformity to rules, customs, or authority with true unity in the Holy Spirit. A group may appear to be very united, while its members are actually discontent or are harboring divisive thoughts.

When symptoms of division appear, the members of the group must prayerfully and honestly seek the cause of the problem. They must ask the Holy Spirit for wisdom to know the causes of the disunity, as well as the ways in which it might best be healed. Again, like a physical disease, the spiritual sickness of disunity requires an accurate diagnosis in order for the proper remedy to be prescribed and applied.

It is easy, for example, to say, "There are seeds of division among us, therefore let's start working as a team." However, if the reasons for the division are not recognized and dealt with, the unity achieved by simply saying (or praying) "Let's be united" will be short lived and illusory.

A group can only discover the causes of tension and disunity by honest discussion and dialogue. This must be done in a context of prayer, asking the light of the Holy Spirit to see what is wrong and the love of the Holy Spirit to be patient, humble, forbearing, and forgiving. All parties must be ready both to acknowledge and repent of their own sin and to take responsibility for the disunity. Most of all, they must be ready to forgive one another. It is evident that such open, honest dialogue leading to reconciliation can only be achieved by a special grace of God and the action of the Holy Spirit. Prayer, seeking only God's will ("Thy will be done"), is therefore absolutely essential.

The church's ministry is a ministry of reconciliation—reconciling people to God and reconciling them to one another. As St. Paul said,

> All this is from God, who through Christ reconciled us to himself, and gave us the ministry of reconciliation; that is, God was in Christ reconciling the world to himself, not counting their trespasses against them, and entrusting to us the message of reconciliation. So we are ambassadors for Christ, God making his appeal through us. We beseech you on behalf of Christ, be reconciled to God. (2 Corinthians 5:18-20)

Reconciliation is the ministry of Jesus, who did not come to condemn the world but to save it; who did not come to divide people but to gather them together in the power of the Holy Spirit into the unity of the church, and to teach those within the church to forgive others as God has forgiven us in Christ.

Nevertheless, reconciliation flies in the face of the "wisdom" of the world today. The world tells married couples considering divorce to consider first their own rights and best interests. The church must remind them of the sacredness of their vows of unity and commitment to each other, and help them to forgive and be reconciled.

The world tells groups and individuals who have a grievance against one another to stand up for their rights and to protest and sue until they are satisfied that they have been vindicated or repaid in full. The church, while supporting the demands of true justice, teaches the lesson of Jesus Christ, who was unjustly condemned and crucified and yet cried out from the cross, "Father, forgive them." St. Paul, writing from a prison cell and persecuted simply because of his faith, instructed the Philippians,

> Do nothing from selfishness or conceit, but in humility count others better than yourselves. Let each of you look not only to his own interests, but also to the interests of others. Have this mind among yourselves, which was in Christ Jesus. (Philippians 2:3-5)

Paul followed this instruction with the powerful hymn to Christ's total self-emptying *(kenosis)* out of love for the world. Paul's aim was to be at peace with all people for the sake of Christ, who gave himself up as an offering for our reconciliation to God.

The world tells Christians who have been hurt by misunderstandings in a Christian group, or by the sin and wrongdoing of other Christians, to break away and to seek their own healing, without reconciliation. But the church is called to administer healing based on forgiveness and reconciliation—as Pope John Paul II illustrated when he met with the man who had shot him, and warmly forgave him from the heart.

The work of the Holy Spirit is to empower the Christian to live the Lord's Prayer, which tells us to forgive those who trespass against us. This is necessary because the church is made up of sinners. The earthly church is necessarily imperfect. Its members will hurt each other through misunderstanding and through offenses, either intentional or unintentional. Hence, one of the greatest works of the Holy Spirit is to preserve and restore unity in the church through forgiveness and reconciliation. Jesus taught his followers to extend unlimited forgiveness, forgiving one another not seven times but seventy times seven times. (Every married couple knows how necessary this is!)

The power to forgive was given to the church and its members by Jesus, as he hung on the cross. The first fruit of Calvary can be seen in John's gospel, when Jesus appeared to his disciples and immediately breathed on them, saying, "Receive the Holy Spirit. If you forgive the sins of any, they are forgiven" (John 20:22-23). Through the Holy Spirit, the successors of the apostles and all who share in Christ's ministerial priesthood receive the commission and authority to forgive sins in Jesus' name and to reconcile people to God and to one another. And through the Holy Spirit, all Christians receive the commission and the power to forgive others and to be reconciled.

Forgiveness is not easy; it is a grace, a gift that is possible only through the power of the blood of Christ, which washes away our sins and heals our wounds. It is possible only through the living water of the Holy Spirit, who empowers us to forgive others and to become one with them and with God.

Ministers of Reconciliation

Practically speaking, Catholic groups do not have to seek to overcome difficulties and divisions on their own; they can call on the pastors of the church to help them in this. The Catholic Church and other Christian churches are greatly aided in the process of reconciliation by the gift of the church's leaders. As we have seen in the Acts of the Apostles, when certain issues threatened to divide the church in Jerusalem (see Acts 6) and the universal church (see Acts 15), it was the elders of the church (the apostles and, later, the bishops) who came together to pray and to settle the issues in a way that would preserve unity. In this they followed the example of Jesus, the good shepherd, who always wished his flock to be united and would even go after the one who went astray. At the end of St. John's gospel, Jesus entrusted the care and unity of his flock, the church, in a special way to Peter (see John 21:15-17). All of the "shepherds" or "pastors" of the church share in Jesus' "pastoral" work of keeping his followers united in faith, hope, and love. The leaders of the church carry out Christ's ministry of reconciliation in a special way. They work by the power and guidance of the Holy Spirit to give direction and to promote or restore unity through forgiveness and reconciliation. Indeed, preserving the unity of the whole body of Christ and of particular groups and communities within the body is the special role and charism of the church's leaders, particularly the bishops. As Pope Paul VI explained to the first International Catholic Charismatic Leaders' Conference in 1973,

> Even in the best experiences of renewal, moreover, weeds may be found among the good seed. So the work of discernment is indispensable; it devolves upon those who are in charge of the Church, those "to whose special competence it belongs, not indeed to extinguish the Spirit, but to test all things and hold fast to that which is good" (cf. 1 Thess. 5:15, 19-21). In this way the common good of the Church, to which the gifts of the Spirit are ordained, is fostered (cf.1 Corinthians. 12:7).[6]

In spite of the difficulty of maintaining or restoring unity in Christ, there is great hope, for the Holy Spirit has been sent by Jesus Christ to make the church and its members ever more fully united in faith, hope, and love. The Holy

Spirit is the binding force, the divine "glue," as it were, who keeps the church united and who alone has the power to overcome the obstacles to unity thrown up by our own human weakness and Satan and the demonic world opposed to God's kingdom.

In the final analysis, we must trust entirely in Jesus' high priestly prayer for unity:

> The glory which thou hast given me I have given to them, that they may be one even as we are one, I in them and thou in me, that they may become perfectly one, so that the world may know that thou hast sent me and hast loved them even as thou hast loved me. . . . O righteous Father, the world has not known thee, but I have known thee, and these know that thou hast sent me. I made known to them thy name, and I will make it known, that the love with which thou hast loved me may be in them, and I in them. (John 17:22-23, 25-26)

The love that set Jesus' heart aflame to pray this prayer and that united him perfectly with the Father is none other than the Holy Spirit. He is the love of God who draws all followers of Christ into perfect unity with each other through their unity in the Father and the Son.

CHAPTER TEN

The Spouse of the Holy Spirit

What does Mary teach us about the Holy Spirit? What is her relationship with him? Like all Christians, Mary is a "temple of the Holy Spirit" who dwells in her, but more than any other person except Jesus, Mary knows the Spirit and his power. Only Mary may be called the "spouse of the Holy Spirit." Only her union with the Holy Spirit brought forth the Son of God, Jesus Christ, into the world in physical, incarnate form.

In spite of this fruitful harmony between Mary and the Holy Spirit, some Christians have difficulty understanding their relationship. Some Catholics with deep Marian devotion do not understand Mary as the ultimate example of a Spirit-filled and Spirit-led Christian, and may even reject any particular devotion to the Holy Spirit. Many Christians with great devotion to and zeal for the Holy Spirit and the Spirit-filled Christian life see no particular need to learn about the Spirit from Mary or to seek her powerful intercession and loving care. Most Protestant Christians regard any prayer or devotion to Mary as idolatry.

Some Christians are confused about who has priority—Mary or the Holy Spirit? Does the Holy Spirit lead us to Mary, or does Mary lead us to the Holy Spirit? (Or is the role of both to lead us to Jesus and the Father?)

There are disputes over what Mary and the Holy Spirit teach us about prayer and Christian life. Mary, it is said, teaches us quiet contemplative prayer, while prayer "in the Spirit" tends to be exterior, vocal, and exuberant; Mary shows us the humble, hidden life of Nazareth, while the Holy

Spirit stirs up missionary activism and evangelization out in the world. How do we resolve these apparent differences?

It should be obvious that in God's mind, there is no conflict or opposition between Mary and the Holy Spirit. The idea is absurd. God must either laugh or cry over the petty disputes between Christians who consider themselves to be either "Marian" *or* "Spirit-filled, charismatic, Pentecostal"— but *not* both. God's revelation in sacred Scripture and Christian tradition explodes these false ideas, as we shall see.

Does Mary point to the Holy Spirit and foster devotion to him? Of course. The Holy Spirit is God, and Mary is a creature, although a creature who was miraculously freed from sin and who exalts God in a unique and powerful way. At the annunciation, Mary's readiness to accept and bear Jesus— her *fiat,* or yes, to God's plan—was also an unconditional yes to receive the Holy Spirit, to allow the Holy Spirit to "overshadow" her to bring forth Jesus (see Luke 1:35-38).

As the *shekinah* cloud of glory overshadowed the ark of the covenant in the Old Testament, the glory of God, the Holy Spirit, overshadowed Mary and made her the Mother of God, the new ark of the covenant. The old ark housed manna, commandments and a staff; the new ark of Mary's womb bore the eternal, divine Son of God, the bread of life.

The *Catechism* explains that Mary, the all-holy and ever-virgin mother of God, is "the masterwork of the mission of the Son and the Spirit in the fullness of time" (721). She was a "first" in God's plan of salvation. Because the Holy Spirit had prepared her, the Father found Mary a fitting dwelling place where his Son and his Spirit could dwell among human beings. The teaching of the Scripture and the church's tradition about the abode of wisdom are now understood more fully in relation to Mary. Mary is acclaimed and represented in the liturgy as the Seat of Wisdom (721).

In his role as the Sanctifier, the one who makes people holy, the Holy Spirit was present to fully sanctify Mary at the moment of her own immaculate conception. What happens to Christians at baptism—being cleansed from sin by the living water of the Spirit and being filled with God's new, abundant life—must have happened to Mary when she was conceived. How else would she have been sanctified as a spotless vessel prepared to bear and bring forth God himself into our world? How else but through the power of the Holy Spirit could Mary have persevered in absolute holiness and dedication to God from the moment of her conception, to her young adulthood (when Jesus was conceived in her), and to the end of her life on earth? Mary is the model of holiness through the work of the Holy Spirit, the Sanctifier, who gave her this unique grace of holiness, freeing her throughout her life from all stain of sin.

It is notable that in the Bible, Gabriel greeted Mary by saying, "Hail, full of grace . . ." *before* she had said yes to God's plan and had been overshadowed by the Holy Spirit. Therefore, Mary must have been "full of grace," and hence filled with the Holy Spirit, even before her "espousal" to the Holy Spirit to bring forth Jesus.

You might say that Mary was baptized with the Holy Spirit at the moment of her conception. Then, at the moment she said yes to God, she became both the bride of the Holy Spirit and, through him, the mother of Jesus. Jesus began to dwell within Mary at the moment the Holy Spirit overshadowed her at the annunciation.[1]

The Holy Spirit's Presence in Mary's Life

What we know about Mary from the Scriptures also tells us about the operation of the Holy Spirit in her life. The action of the Holy Spirit makes her unique and special in

God's plan of salvation. In the scene in Luke's gospel following the annunciation, Mary rose and visited her cousin Elizabeth. Elizabeth was an older, barren woman who had also miraculously conceived by God's power. When Mary greeted Elizabeth, "the babe leaped in her womb, and Elizabeth was filled with the Holy Spirit and she exclaimed with a loud cry, 'Blessed are you among women, and blessed is the fruit of your womb!'" (Luke 1:40-42).

Elizabeth's reaction to seeing her cousin reveals an important truth about Mary: her presence evokes the presence of the Holy Spirit in others. When Elizabeth heard Mary, John the Baptist leapt in his mother's womb, and Elizabeth was "filled with the Holy Spirit" and immediately uttered a prophecy. Something similar happened when Jesus was presented in the temple. When Simeon, who had been "inspired by the Spirit" to come to the temple, saw Joseph, Mary, and the child Jesus there, he took Jesus in his arms and burst into a prophetic prayer of praise. He then turned to Mary and prophesied about her son and about the sword that would pierce her own soul so that the thoughts of many hearts might be revealed. Anna, an elderly prophet, also approached the Holy Family, gave thanks to God, and "spoke of [the child] to all who were looking for the redemption of Jerusalem" (see Luke 2:22-38).

The presence of the Holy Spirit in Mary is obvious not only in others' reactions to her but also in her own words. Her Magnificat (Luke 1:46-55) is one of the most beautiful prophetic prayers of praise recorded in sacred Scripture. Anyone who thinks that Mary is a pure contemplative who did not proclaim spontaneous, "charismatic" prayers in praise of God has forgotten the Magnificat!

But, Mary was also a contemplative. Luke observes that, as angels appeared and shepherds came to adore Jesus at his birth, Mary "kept all these things, pondering them in her heart" (Luke 2:19). The word "pondering" is also used to describe Mary when she found Jesus in the temple after his disappearance at age twelve. Pondering is a contemplative activity.

When we think of contemplative prayer, we are tempted to think of someone locked in a chapel, praying constantly, with nothing ever really happening to them. Contemplation can appear to be something abstract or detached from life. Mary was not that kind of contemplative; she pondered actions of the Holy Spirit that she experienced in the events of her life.

And what exactly is pondering? Fr. Bertrand Buby, a noted Mariologist, observes that while it does involve wondering or being amazed, pondering is more than that: Mary "is interpreting and turning over in her heart and memory the meaning of God's salvific action among her people." It is a calm and joyful prayer, a treasuring of the mystery of God's actions and an attempt "to fathom the mysteries of God within her and those which surround her, reflecting upon the meaning of her Son who is Savior and Messiah Lord. She does not solve the mystery. She simply ponders."[2]

For Mary, prayer is a work of the Holy Spirit that is sometimes vocal, prophetic, and praise-filled, and sometimes a contemplative pondering of the mystery of God and his saving acts. Mary's pondering of God's words and works is an expression of two of the gifts of the Spirit listed by Isaiah: wisdom and understanding.

Mary's Motherhood in the Spirit

In Luke's gospel, we have seen Mary praying in praise and prophecy and in contemplative pondering. In the Acts of the Apostles, Luke portrays Mary as the powerful intercessor who prayed for the Holy Spirit to be poured out upon all Jesus' followers and upon the whole world. We see Mary joined in intercessory prayer with the whole Christian community of 120 people who are gathered in the upper room: "All these with one accord devoted themselves to prayer, together with the women and Mary the mother of Jesus, and with his brethren" (Acts 1:14).

Pope John Paul II calls our attention to the power of Mary's intercession and her special role of "motherhood in the Spirit," giving birth both to the physical body of Jesus at the incarnation and to his spiritual body, the church, at Pentecost. Reflecting on Acts 1:14, John Paul II wrote in his encyclical letter on Mary, *Redemptoris Mater,*

> In the redemptive economy of grace, brought about through the action of the Holy Spirit, there is a unique correspondence between the moment of the incarnation of the Word and the moment of the birth of the Church. The person who links these two moments is Mary: Mary at Nazareth and Mary in the upper room at Jerusalem. In both cases her discreet yet essential presence indicates the path of "birth from the Holy Spirit." Thus she who is present in the mystery of Christ as Mother becomes—by the will of the Son and the power of the Holy Spirit—present in the mystery of the Church.[3]

Pope John Paul II alludes to one of the two places where Mary is prominent in the Gospel of John. The first is at the wedding feast at Cana, where we also see the power of Mary's intercession as she prevails upon her Son to work his first miracle. Mary is led by the Holy Spirit to make this bold request, though in such a humble way: "Do whatever he tells you" (John 2:5). The water of the old covenant begins to give way to the wine of the new through Mary's intercession.

We also see Mary mourning and praying at the foot of the cross of her Son. In the fourth gospel, Mary, John and the women who are gathered at the foot of the cross represent the church (see John 19:25). It is at this moment that Jesus gives Mary to us as mother of the church. As Pope John Paul II put it, "In the Church too [Mary] continues to be a maternal presence as is shown by the words spoken from the Cross: "Woman behold your Son!"; "Behold, your mother." In John's theology, the Holy Spirit is also released upon the church as Jesus is glorified in his death. Blood and water, representing the Spirit, flow from Jesus' pierced side. (Later Catholic writers equated the blood and water with baptism and the Eucharist, but the earliest Christian writers saw the water flowing from Jesus' side as the "living water" of the Spirit, which is indeed normally first given in baptism). As in Luke's gospel, Mary is present in prayer at this symbolic moment of the sending of the Holy Spirit to the church.

Because of Mary's special role as mother of the church, it is especially appropriate for us to pray to her and to see her as a model for our own prayer. The *Catechism* explains,

> When we pray to [Mary], we are adhering with her to the plan of the Father, who sends his Son to save all men. Like the beloved disciple we welcome Jesus' mother into our homes, for she has become the mother of all the living. We can pray with and to her. The prayer of the Church is sustained by the prayer of Mary and united with it in hope (2679).

Where Mary Is, There Is the Holy Spirit

One conclusion I would draw from the biblical evidence about Mary is simply that *where Mary is, there is the Holy*

Spirit! Whether it be through her intercession or simply through her presence, Mary, in whom the Holy Spirit dwells in a special way, evokes the Holy Spirit in others.

The intercession of Mary and the other disciples reported in Acts 1:14 resulted in the universal outpouring of the Holy Spirit on all Jesus' followers, that is, on the whole church. This was the day of Pentecost, ushered in by the sound of a mighty rushing wind and tongues as of fire resting on each one in the room: "And they were all filled with the Holy Spirit and began to speak in other tongues, as the Spirit gave them utterance" (Acts 2:3-4).

Another conclusion we can draw about Mary and the Holy Spirit is that *Mary possessed a rich abundance of the gifts and charisms of the Holy Spirit.* Acts 1:14 includes Mary among those present at Pentecost who were filled with the Holy Spirit and spoke in tongues. Mary was a "tongues-speaking, charismatic Christian."[4]

And as we have seen, Mary was also a *prophet:* "All generations will call me blessed," she prophesied in her Magnificat (Luke 1:48). She was known to have burst into spontaneous prayers of praise to God, as Jesus sometimes did (see Luke 10:21-22). Mary also had the gift of contemplative prayer and adoration. In *Marialis Cultus,* Pope Paul VI reported that "some fathers and writers of the church" saw the Holy Spirit as the source of Mary's many gifts:

Delving deeply into the doctrine of the Paraclete, they saw that from him as from a spring there flowed forth the fullness of grace (Luke 1:28) and the abundance of gifts that adorned her. Thus they attributed to the Spirit the faith, hope and charity that animated the Virgin's heart, the strength that sustained her acceptance of the will of God, and the vigor that upheld her in her suffering at the foot of the Cross . . . In Mary's prophetic canticle (Luke 1:46-55) they saw a special working of the Spirit who had spoken through the mouths of the prophets.[5]

The New Testament portrait of Mary reveals a person who is totally open and responsive to the teachings and gifts of the Holy Spirit. As the noted Marian scholar Frederick M. Jelly has written,

> Mary is the model charismatic. . . . Mary herself is one of the great gifts of the Spirit to us. In the continuous Pentecost of the church's history she is called to give us the greatest example of responding to the gifts and charisms of the Spirit for the sake of the church. In Mary we behold the most marvelous manifestation of the Spirit who touches each one of us personally to bring out what is best in our own personalities for the sake of the community.[6]

Mary didn't place any limitations on the working of God in her life. Even when she didn't understand certain actions, such as the initial gift of her Son's incarnation, she accepted them. Even when she didn't fully understand why her Son left the family to remain in Jerusalem, or why he was rejected by his own neighbors and kin, or why he had to be rejected by the Jewish people and suffer and die, Mary continued to ponder these things and to pray. Moreover, she didn't judge the other followers of Jesus who had abandoned him at the cross or who, like Thomas, had doubted his resurrection. Rather, she remained with them, praying for them all to receive the fullness of the Holy Spirit, just as she had.

Thus, Mary deeply understood the Spirit as God's own generous, merciful, persevering love poured into her heart (see Romans 5:5)—a love that expressed itself in praying for the Christian community and lovingly using her gifts for the strengthening of the community of her Son. Through the Spirit of love that she possessed in fullness, Mary fulfills her role as the heart and the mother of the church.

Mary in God's Plan of Salvation

To fully understand Mary's role in God's plan of salvation, it is important to see her not as an isolated individual but in relationship to her son and as a member of the Spirit-filled, charismatic community Jesus founded. The relationship of Mary to Jesus has often been commented on: Mary is not a deity; her dignity flows from her role in God's plan of salvation, particularly her role as the mother of God the Son. Mary's greatest desire, then and now, was and is to lead people to Jesus.

However, we tend to forget that Mary must also be seen and related to as a Christian, a fellow member of the church. True, she is the church's most exalted member. (She who was most humble and docile to the Spirit on earth has become the most honored in heaven.) But at the same time, Mary is "one of us"—a point that the council fathers of Vatican II stressed by consciously deciding not to issue a separate document on her. And so Vatican II's fullest teaching on Mary is the final chapter of its "Dogmatic Constitution on the Church."

The last glimpses we have of Mary in the New Testament also indicate Mary's relationship with the church. In John's gospel, Mary is at the foot of the cross, with John and the other women. From the cross Jesus declares her to be the mother of the beloved disciple and, symbolically, of the whole community of "beloved disciples" gathered for all ages around the cross. This is the fulfillment of Jesus' mission, "to gather into one the scattered children of God" (John 11:52) and of his promise, "I, when I am lifted up from the earth, will draw all men to myself" (John 12:32). Mary is portrayed in John's gospel as the mother of this new community that gathers first around the cross of Jesus and extends eventually to the ends of the earth. It is a community bound together in unity by the love of God, the Holy Spirit.

In the Acts of the Apostles, our last glimpse of Mary is at Pentecost, when she gathered with her son's community in prayer as they received the greatest gift that Jesus promised: the Holy Spirit. What happened there was obviously the fulfillment of Jesus' promise: Mary and the disciples were "baptized in the Holy Spirit." The sign of this baptism was that they received charisms, or gifts of the Holy Spirit: "They were all filled with the Holy Spirit and began to speak in other tongues, as the Spirit gave them utterance" (Acts 2:4). Then they went out proclaiming the good news in power, and thousands were converted (see Acts 2:41, 47; 4:24, 30; 9:31).

Since the Holy Spirit had been poured out and active in Mary's life from the beginning, can we say that Mary was baptized in the Spirit at Pentecost? And what about the apostles? Had they not received the Holy Spirit again after Pentecost? I would agree with the analysis of Fr. René Laurentin:

Mary, who had already been filled with the Holy Spirit at the annunciation, when the Holy Spirit came upon her, received at Pentecost a new fullness. The first fullness does not make the second unnecessary. In the same way, the apostles who were "filled with the Holy Spirit" (Acts 2:4) at Pentecost were filled anew with the Spirit at the new Pentecost, given to them to rise above the shock of the first persecution.

"And when they had prayed, the place in which they were gathered together was shaken; and they were all filled with the Holy Spirit and spoke the word of God with boldness" (Acts 4:31).

All of them were already filled; they are filled anew, in new dimensions of their existence. And this too is what happens to Mary—to establish in her the new relationship with the Holy Spirit, in keeping with the new status and the new mission of the church, constituted at that moment. Mary was its prototype. She becomes a member of it, and a spiritual leader.[7]

Fr. Laurentin's position is convincing because it respects Jesus' own prophecy that soon his disciples would be "baptized with the Holy Spirit" (Acts 1:5). It also agrees with the testimony of the Acts of the Apostles and the constant experience of the life of the church that the Holy Spirit is not limited to a single "coming": the Spirit may come *many* times into the life of the individual and the community to refresh, renew, and deepen his work and to grant new charisms. We see this exemplified in the life of Mary, whom the Holy Spirit blessed in significant ways at her own immaculate conception, at the annunciation, and at Pentecost. The early church, too, experienced many new sendings of the Spirit: at the first great Pentecost (see Acts 2); at the "little" Pentecost (see Acts 4:29-31); and at many other "Pentecosts"—at Cornelius' house (see Acts 10:16-17), in Samaria (see Acts 8:14-17), in Ephesus (see Acts 19:1-7), and so on. In each case, it may be appropriate to say that God has "baptized" the person or group "with the Holy Spirit."

Fr. Laurentin thinks that we have complicated the issue by focusing on the terminology rather than on the reality. He comments,

Every fervent Christian life is constituted by the outpouring of the Spirit renewed again and again, which at times may take the form of a Pentecost. This outpouring is a communication of the life of God, i.e., of *agape,* of charity, or if you like, of grace, through the person of the Spirit himself—a spring of living water welling up to eternal life. Having said that, it does not matter whether we say "baptism" or "outpouring" of the Spirit. . . . It does not matter whether this outpouring precedes baptism, as in the case of many catechumens, or follows it, as in the case of most of us.[8]

Certainly, the Acts of the Apostles demonstrates, as at Cornelius' house, that the outpouring or baptism of the Holy Spirit could occur at any time, before or after baptism. The Book of Acts accentuates the freedom of the Spirit, which "blows where it wills" (John 3:8). Acts also insists that baptism in water is essential for full Christian initiation, but that Christian initiation is not complete until the Holy Spirit is poured out and manifested by the spiritual gifts, or charisms.[9]

Returning to Mary, we simply claim that she interceded for the Spirit's coming and experienced afresh being baptized in the Holy Spirit at Pentecost, because she belonged to the community, the church, that was raised up by the Holy Spirit and lived by the Spirit. This primitive church was a charismatic community, since the gifts of the Holy Spirit were normal and essential to its life.[10] It was truly a Spirit-filled community.

It is impressive to note how many times the Acts of the Apostles describes the church or particular individuals in it as being *full of* or *filled with* the Holy Spirit (see, for example, Acts 2:4; 4:8, 31; 6:3, 5, 10; 7:55; 9:17; 10:44; 11:24; 13:9, 52). In Scripture, this designation is a supreme compliment, and Peter, Paul, Stephen, and Barnabas are among the individuals so described. Mary, too, is among the foremost members of the primitive church to deserve this title of "Spirit-filled."

Opposition Between Mary and the Holy Spirit?

Someone might observe that in the lives of many prayerful Catholics there is a strong devotion to Mary but less attention to the Holy Spirit. Though these Catholics may have Jesus Christ and the heavenly Father clearly at the center of their lives, with Mary enriching their love of Christ, they often neglect the Holy Spirit in their faith and worship. What should Christians do when devotion and prayer to Mary seem to overshadow love of God, who is Father, Son, and Holy Spirit? How do we know whether such devotion to Mary has become imbalanced or even wrong?

There are obvious reasons why Mary receives more emphasis than the Holy Spirit in the devotion of many Catholics. We know that human persons relate naturally to other *persons.* Christianity is an *incarnational* religion. God knew that we would be drawn closer to him if he entered into our history as a person, Jesus Christ, through the mystery of the incarnation. What a breakthrough for the human race to know God as Emmanuel—"God with us!" What a blessing to see his love for us incarnated, made real to us, in the person of Jesus, especially as he suffered and died for us on Calvary.

Through Jesus, we have also gained a better idea of who God is as our Father. Jesus came explicitly to reveal the Father. He told us about his Father's love and mercy in the beautiful parable of the prodigal son. He said to Philip, "He who has seen me has seen the Father" (John 14:9). The works, love, and judgments of the Father are all revealed perfectly in his Son, Jesus.

Jesus also came to announce to his disciples the great gift that he and the Father would send them, so that they would look forward to it eagerly and receive it gratefully. No, this gift was not Mary! Nowhere in Scripture did Jesus *prepare* the disciples for the gift of Mary; he simply gave her to John from the cross as his mother, and our mother, as his last living act. Perhaps Jesus needed to explain the gift of the Holy Spirit more to his disciples so that they could understand and relate to the Spirit properly. One doesn't have to explain the role of a mother.

In any case, Jesus described the gift of the Holy Spirit as the "promise of my Father" and "power from on high" (Luke 24:49). He told his apostles about the "Spirit of truth" (John 14:17) who would lead and guide them and give them words to say when they were brought before governors and kings (see Matthew 10:18-20). He called the Spirit the Counselor, or Advocate (see John 14:25), "rivers of living water" welling up to eternal life (John 7:38-39).

But despite Jesus' description of this greatest of gifts, the average person still finds it easier to relate in a *personal* way to Mary than to the Holy Spirit. Mary is a mother, a model mother of mercy and compassion. The Holy Spirit remains somewhat faceless and elusive. It is difficult to have a close personal relationship with this person of the Trinity who is imagined primarily as an impersonal force, like the biblical images of wind and fire or as the peaceful dove or as the "still small voice" that nudges the conscience. That is why I think it is easier to have a devotion to the person of Mary, our mother, than to the Holy Spirit, and why it is easier to pray to Mary, who is a redeemed human being, than to the Holy Spirit, who is God.

Nonetheless, this difficulty *can* be overcome. And it should be faced, for there is a problem if Christians feel, for any reason, that they cannot or should not approach

God—the Father, the Son, or the Holy Spirit. Devotion to Mary and the saints is all directed to leading Christians into a deeper relationship of praise, worship, love, and service of God. Consequently, knowledge and love of Mary should ultimately lead us to know and love God more. As Pope Paul VI put it, "Our primary devotion should be to the Holy Spirit (to which devotion to the Blessed Virgin leads us, as it leads us to Christ!)"[11]

Pray and Listen

One way to seek a relationship with the Holy Spirit is to address him and speak of him as a person. This may seem awkward to some Catholics, because we tend to think of the Holy Spirit in *non*personal ways—as fire, wind, water, etc. But as we have seen from our review of the person of the Holy Spirit in the New Testament, before Mary was ever addressed in prayer, it was normal and natural to relate to and speak of the Holy Spirit as a person.

The New Testament clearly describes the Holy Spirit as a person who guides, directs, and speaks to the church. Unfortunately, as the Spirit says through the prophet Isaiah (see 6:9-10; Acts 28:25-27), the people's hearts have grown dull and their ears heavy. Most Christians today do not believe that the Holy Spirit is a person who can guide, teach, and speak to them as he did in the New Testament.

In the second and third centuries, the danger was that Christians might fall into heresies such as Montanism, which overemphasized spiritual experience and led to harmful and erroneous interpretations of the Holy Spirit's voice. Today the danger is that Christians will go to the other extreme and not expect the Holy Spirit ever to address them personally. They assume that the Spirit will speak only through the official doctrines of the church, through the clergy or magisterium, through widely recognized approved prophetic figures, and through sacred Scripture and tradition. Many Catholics think that Marian messages and apparitions are the primary way that the Holy Spirit speaks to the church.

There is no doubt that the Holy Spirit speaks through the Bible, sacred tradition, and official church doctrines. It is also true that the Holy Spirit continues to speak through the prophetic gift and prophetic figures in the church. Mary, as a prophet and a proclaimer of the good news, is prominent among these figures.

However, we must not deny the possibility—indeed, the reality—of the Holy Spirit's speaking to and guiding individual Christians today, as he did in New Testament times. This requires developing a sensitivity to the voice of the Spirit, an art that normally comes through *prayer*. Usually, only the prayerful person who is listening for the words and guidance of the Holy Spirit will receive them.

Where can we learn to hear the voice of the Holy Spirit? *Who* can teach us what it means to relate to the Holy Spirit as a person? I suggest turning to Scripture to find the best instructors—the Old Testament prophets, for example. Their stories tell of women and men who regularly received God's word and wisdom for his people. In the Nicene Creed, Christians profess the faith of the early church that the Holy Spirit "has spoken through the prophets." From these biblical prophets we receive Spirit-inspired words of truth for all time. We can also study their example of how they listened and responded to the voice of the Holy Spirit in their particular circumstances.

Of course, Jesus teaches us about listening and responding to the Holy Spirit. His entire life and ministry were guided by and filled with the Spirit, whose voice he always heard and obeyed and in whose power he preached and acted. The Son of God's ministry on earth was to proclaim and bring forth

God's kingdom through the guidance and power of the Holy Spirit. We can *learn* when Jesus "rejoice[s] in the Holy Spirit" (Luke 10:21-22) and *listen* when he tells us when and how the Holy Spirit will teach and guide us, so that we may come to *believe* in his words and *follow* his example.

We may also learn from saints like Paul, who were especially responsive to the Holy Spirit and conversed with him. And it is obvious that Mary, as the "spouse of the Holy Spirit," has much to teach us. We know from Scripture that Mary was filled with the Holy Spirit in a remarkable and unique way. We have seen how she pondered his action in the events of her life. Therefore, it is instructive to think about Mary's own words and actions as the fruit of that pondering—her visit to her cousin Elizabeth during her pregnancy; her request that Jesus supply more wine at Cana; her endurance of persecution, trial, and misunderstanding as she followed Jesus even to the foot of the cross. From all the events of Mary's life, we learn what it means to be in a close relationship with the Holy Spirit and how to follow his lead.

Jesus and Mary: To See Them Is to See the Spirit

If we are really serious about getting to know the Holy Spirit as a person, we should take an even closer look at the lives of Jesus and Mary. In them, we see the Spirit in a special way.

Jesus, in his life and teaching, most fully reveals the Holy Spirit to us. Just as Jesus said to Philip that to see him was to see the Father, I think it would also be true, though in a slightly different way, to say that to see Jesus is to see the Holy Spirit. The three persons of the blessed Trinity are perfectly one. Jesus, as the incarnate Son and Word of God, is the perfect image of the Father. And Jesus can only act according to the will and power, the love and truth of the Holy Spirit. Everything Jesus says and does manifests perfectly both the person of the Father and the person of the Holy Spirit.

In coming to know Jesus, we come to know the very Spirit who brings forth in the Messiah all the messianic gifts listed by the prophet Isaiah. In Jesus we encounter the Spirit of Truth, the all-consuming love of God, the power of God—the source of every gift in the body of Christ and the ultimate expression of God's unity and holiness.

We also see the Holy Spirit in Mary, who is his spouse and temple. Though Scripture never presents her as speaking directly about the Holy Spirit, Mary reveals him in a powerful way, because she is full of the Spirit and led by the Spirit more completely than any person except her divine Son. The work of the Spirit in her is not impeded by any sin. Some authors, such as St. Maximilian Kolbe, have called Mary the *quasi incarnatus* (quasi-incarnation) of the Holy Spirit. St. Maximilian explained the relationship this way:

> It is said that the Holy Spirit dwells in the souls of the just. If this is so, then he must dwell in the most perfect manner possible in the soul of the Immaculata. Our most Holy Mother is totally suffused with the divine. . . . The third person of the blessed Trinity never took flesh; still, our human word "spouse" is far too weak to express the reality of the relationship between the Immaculata and the Holy Spirit. We can affirm that she is, in a certain sense, the "incarnation" of the Holy Spirit. It is the Holy Spirit that we love in her; and through her we love the Son.[12]

Fr. H. M. Manteau-Bonamy explains these statements in his book, *Immaculate Conception and the Holy Spirit:*

Between Mary the Immaculata and the Holy Spirit there is a deep union not only because Mary's will is absolutely conformed with that of the Holy Spirit, as a dutiful spouse's would be, and also because she was always a conscious and free instrument in his regard, a true handmaid, but more precisely because the Holy Spirit dwells in her as in his privileged *sanctuary*.[13]

The Second Vatican Council described Mary as "the mother of God's Son, and as a consequence, . . . the Father's well-beloved daughter and the *sanctuary of the Holy Spirit*."[14]

Fr. Manteau-Bonamy refines the metaphor further:

To understand better what this indwelling of the Holy Spirit in Mary means, think of a vase placed right in the heart of a bubbling spring. Not only does the vase fill with water; it overflows. . . . Mary, the Immaculata, united to the Holy Spirit, communicates to us this living water which refreshes all those who consecrate themselves to their Mother in the Spirit.[15]

In Mary, Christians can see the presence and action of the Holy Spirit with power and perfect clarity. Through Mary's intercession, the church and each Christian can receive an abundant outpouring of the living water of the Spirit, a renewal of the grace of the first Pentecost that came as a result of Mary's intercession with Jesus' disciples.

Catholic theology and doctrine proclaim that Mary, as the exemplary disciple of Jesus, is the foremost model of the church. In her reception of the Holy Spirit at her conception and at the annunciation, she prefigures the gift of the Holy Spirit to the entire church at Pentecost. Both Mary and the church are first *recipients* and *sanctuaries* of God's gift of the Spirit, then *models* or *examples* of completely Spirit-filled and Spirit-led Christian existences, and finally *channels* through whose prayers and witnesses the Holy Spirit is born and renewed in the lives of others. Let us constantly pray, with the church and Mary, "Come Holy Spirit! Fill the hearts of your faithful and enkindle in us the fire of your love!"

We have seen in this chapter that Mary is a woman whose heart was aflame with a passionate, persevering love of God. She was a woman of prayer who allowed the Holy Spirit to speak to her in the depths of her being, until her heart welled up with praise and thanksgiving to God: "My soul proclaims the greatness of the Lord." Having received the Holy Spirit from the moment of her own conception, freeing her from original sin, Mary continued to say yes to God throughout her life. When she said yes to the archangel Gabriel, the Holy Spirit was able to overshadow her to conceive the Son of God in her womb. Wherever Mary went, her mere presence called forth a movement or action of the Holy Spirit in others, like her cousin Elizabeth. The climax of the work of the Holy Spirit through Mary was her presence with the apostles on the eve of Pentecost. It was through Mary's yes that the Old Testament prophecies of the people were at last *fulfilled!*

My prayer is that just as Mary's presence called forth the Holy Spirit in power at Pentecost, so too her intercession would bring forth the great work of God's holy church. May the Lord, through Mary's powerful intercession, bless the church with a "new Pentecost," a new and powerful outpouring of the Holy Spirit in the church and in the world today.

"Spirit-Filled" Worship in the Catholic Tradition

F ew Catholics realize that some aspects of modern-day "Spirit-filled" or "charismatic" worship closely resemble Christian worship in the first two or three centuries after Christ. Two prominent outward features of this form of worship today are the prayer posture of lifted arms and hands, and praying or singing with the gift of tongues.

Praying with raised or upturned hands was apparently common in the first centuries of Christianity. The *orans* or "pray-er" with hands raised is a familiar figure in the frescoes of the Roman catacombs (of St. Priscilla, St. Callistus, and others). Many of these frescoes portray figures from the Old Testament praising God with raised hands for his mighty acts in delivering Israel; they also portray Christians of their day, such as St. Cecilia, praying with upraised arms. In his treatise *On Baptism*, Tertullian, a church father of the third century, instructs the neophytes (the newly baptized):

> When you come up from the most sacred bath of the new birth, when you spread out your hands for the first time in your mother's house with your brethren, ask your Father, ask your Lord, for the special gift of his inheritance, the distributed charisms, which form an additional, underlying feature [of baptism]. Ask, he says, and you shall receive.[1]

When the neophytes entered the church ("your mother's house") for the first time after their baptism, they raised their hands in prayer and asked for the charisms, the gifts of the Holy Spirit. As Fr. Kilian McDonnell explains,

> The posture of standing with arms outstretched and palms open was customary when the community entered into the prayer of praise, in contrast to the penitential prayer made on one's knees.[2]

It is interesting that in the catacombs, few, if any, figures are portrayed kneeling in prayer, while many frescoes show the *orans* with upraised arms, praising God.

Another church father of the third century, Origen, explains in his treatise *On Prayer* that bodily posture reflects the disposition of the soul. He concludes,

> And although there are a great many different positions for the body, he should not doubt that the position with the hands outstretched and the eyes lifted up is to be preferred before all others, because it bears in prayer the image of characteristics befitting the soul and applies it to the body. . . . Kneeling is necessary when someone is going to speak against his own sins before God, since he is making supplication for their healing and their forgiveness.[3]

"Speaking in tongues," or glossolalia, is another dimension of Spirit-filled worship that is deeply rooted in the Catholic tradition. In addition to the testimony of Scripture to glossolalia (St. Paul's letters and the Acts of the Apostles), many of the saints of the early church speak about the prayer of "jubilation" as a gift of inspired, Spirit-filled praise of God. As Eddie Ensley explains in his book, *Sounds of Wonder: A Popular History of Speaking in Tongues in the Catholic Tradition,*

This period of the Fathers was a time of a rich variety of styles of expressive prayer and worship. Perhaps the most significant and fascinating form of spontaneous prayer during the formative period was a form of prayer without words, closely resembling the "tongues" of present-day charismatic renewal, called jubilation. Jubilation was a form of praying and singing aloud without words. Though consciousness of the role that this wordless prayer played in the tradition has grown very dim in the last hundred years, it played a very vital role in the formation of the liturgy till the ninth century and in private prayer till the late Middle Ages, and traces of it can be found in the mystical tradition as late as the nineteenth century.[4]

St. Augustine of Hippo wrote about jubilation in his sermon on Psalm 32, which is appropriately chosen in the Liturgy of the Hours to commemorate the feast of St. Cecilia on November 22. There is a beautiful ancient fresco of St. Cecilia, the patroness of musicians, in the catacombs of St. Callistus. There she is pictured with her arms upraised singing the praise of God in jubilation. St. Augustine wrote,

This is singing well to God, just singing with songs of joy. But how is this done? You must first understand that words cannot express the things that are sung by the heart. Take the case of people singing while harvesting in the fields or in the vineyards or when any other strenuous work is in progress. Although they begin by giving expression to their happiness in sung words, yet shortly there is a change. As if so happy that words can no longer express what they feel, they discard the restricting syllables. They burst out into a simple sound of joy, of jubilation. Such a cry of joy is a sound signifying that the heart is bringing to birth what it cannot utter in words.

Now, who is more worthy of such a cry of jubilation than God himself, whom all words fail to describe? If words will not serve, and yet you must not remain silent, what else can you do but cry out for joy? Your heart must rejoice beyond words, soaring into an immensity of gladness, unrestrained by syllabic bonds. Sing to him with songs of joy.[5]

Who would not welcome such a wonderful gift? And yet, praising God "wordlessly" is not always easy, because it demands openness and responsiveness to God's work and to initiatives of the Holy Spirit that may not be familiar to many Christians today. It is certainly necessary also to discern the Holy Spirit in the beautiful and rich liturgical traditions of the church, and to learn to enter into prayer through these traditions. However, even these traditions need to be continually brought to life by the vivifying action of the Holy Spirit. How many Catholics experience the liturgical life of their parish as routine, dull, or "dead," and sometimes leave to join other Christian churches?

How are we to answer those who say that the liturgy or prayers of the church seem dull or lifeless? Different responses could be made:

1. *The apologetic response.* Some Catholics agree with Pope Benedict XVI's statement, "The life of the liturgy does not consist in 'pleasant' surprises and attractive ideas but in solemn repetitions. It cannot be an expression of what is current and transitory, for it expresses the mystery of the Holy."[6]

Since the Mass and prayer are not meant to be entertainment, these Catholics would insist that if the Mass seems dull, or if personal prayer seems perennially dry, the problem is not with the Mass or the prayer but with the person who has failed to appreciate worship for what it is and to enter into it more fully.

While recognizing the truth of this response, we must also see that it could be used to justify situations that need to be changed. It could easily become a reason for expecting private prayer to be just ritual without any personal contact with God, and for tolerating liturgies that really are dull and seemingly lifeless due to poor leadership on the part of the celebrant or other ministers and to half-hearted participation by the congregation. But if the celebrant and ministers first make an effort to become energized about the liturgy themselves, they will be able to transfer that enthusiasm to the congregation. The Second Vatican Council explained,

> In the restoration and promotion of the sacred liturgy the full and active participation by all the people is the aim to be considered before all else, for it is the primary and indispensable source from which the faithful are to derive the true Christian spirit. Therefore, in all their pastoral activity, pastors of souls should energetically set about achieving it through the requisite pedagogy. . . .
>
> Yet it would be futile to entertain any hope of realizing this unless pastors of souls, in the first place, themselves become fully imbued with the spirit and power of the liturgy and capable of giving instruction about it.[7]

When priests and people are celebrating the liturgy and praying wholeheartedly, according to the church's instruction, no one will be able to call this worship dull or lifeless! The intrinsic beauty, power, and grace of the church's prayer will shine forth brightly, set aflame by the Holy Spirit, who is the source of all true worship.

2. The educational response. This may be seen as a necessary complement to the apologetic response. If the basic problem is that Christians fail to expect much from their prayer and the church's liturgy and fail to enter into these with mind and heart ready to worship God, then some education must be provided. Teaching them about the true nature of the liturgy and prayer will encourage and help them to appreciate these modes of prayer and to enter into them more fully.

To say that worship may be brought alive by such instruction is certainly true. In the Catholic Church, the responsibility for this instruction lies especially with those who lead the community in liturgical worship, the clergy. As Vatican II's "Constitution on the Sacred Liturgy" states,

> With zeal and patience pastors of souls must promote the liturgical instruction of the faithful and also their active participation, both internal and external, taking into account their age, condition, way of life and standard of religious culture. By so doing pastors will be fulfilling one of the chief duties of a faithful dispenser of the mysteries of God, and in this matter they must lead their flock not only by word but also by example.[8]

3. The creative response. This response contends that if the liturgy and prayer seem dull, then we must find creative and innovative ways to make them more attractive and appealing to modern people. Unfortunately, the emphasis here often is not on discovering and unfolding the true nature of the liturgy (or prayer) according to authentic

Christian tradition or the guidelines of the church; rather this approach tends to try to incorporate into the liturgy or prayer whatever new things people today might enjoy or find novel or attractive. The danger of such "creativity" is that prayer and the liturgy may come to be viewed as a purely human enterprise, rather than a response to the Holy Spirit's creative initiative. Without the guidance of the Holy Spirit, some have created prayer forms that reflect mainly their own quest for originality, creativity, or novelty. How many people have been distressed by experiments or innovations in liturgical prayer that have responded more to the "spirit of the age"—what is novel or popular—than to the Holy Spirit!

In extreme cases, some Christians have begun to borrow indiscriminately from other religions and cults or from popular trends in secular culture, instead of recovering and renewing the richness of the Christian tradition. Prayer in such cases becomes the expression of an ideology, or worse, worship of false gods or demons.

The Catholic Church is aware of the need for "inculturation"—the legitimate adaptation of Christian faith to different cultures—but this is essentially a transformation of these cultures through the truth of the gospel. It allows certain cultural forms to be used to increase participation and understanding. An evident example of this is allowing the use of the vernacular, the "language of the people," in liturgical worship, on the principle that "the liturgy is made up of unchangeable elements divinely instituted, and of elements subject to change."[9] Again, it is the role of the official teachers of the church, guided by the Holy Spirit, to determine which elements of liturgy are divinely instituted and which are subject to change:

Regulation of the sacred liturgy depends solely on the authority of the Church, that is on the bishop. Therefore no other person, not even a priest, may add remove, or change anything on his own authority.[10]

4. The renewal response. This final response to the challenge of developing a truly reverent and "alive" worship recognizes the need for our prayer and liturgy to be constantly deepened and made more worshipful through the action of the Holy Spirit. It includes being open to recovering the modes of worship that were common in the early church—such as praying with arms upraised and praying and singing in tongues (jubilation) when appropriate, even in the liturgy. Lifting up our hearts and voices to God can take a visible, incarnational form through these practices, which as we have seen, are a venerable part of our Catholic tradition of worship.

Are the Gifts of the Holy Spirit Practical?

Another way that the Holy Spirit's work could be manifested more richly in the church today would be through a fuller, freer use of the full range of charisms. In principle, there should be no question about the importance for the church of the gifts of the Holy Spirit. Biblically, the New Testament (particularly St. Paul) insists that *all* Christians have gifts from the Holy Spirit and that these are absolutely necessary for the church. The church is Christ's body, which only functions as each member of the body actively uses his or her gifts for the good of the whole body, serving one another in love.

It is indisputable that the church could not function without these gifts. Where would the church be if it lacked pastors, teachers, and administrators? The gifts of pastoring and teaching are necessary for those serving in the ministerial (ordained) priesthood, and yet the church needs laypeople, as well, who have pastoral, teaching, and administrative gifts and who use them in service of the church and in the world.

What would the church be like if it lacked the gifts of service, healing, and generosity in giving aid and alms? The church has a mission of service to the world, which could not be accomplished without the exercise of gifts such as these.

How could the church and its members be guided by Christ and the Holy Spirit without the gifts of knowledge, wisdom, and discernment? If the church were a purely human institution, then purely human reason would be sufficient for decision making and guidance. But since the church is ultimately guided and directed by God working through human instruments, then the gifts of the Holy Spirit, who is given to guide the church into the fullness of truth, are absolutely necessary.

What about other gifts of guidance, such as prophecy, the prophetic gift of tongues and the interpretation of tongues, and discernment of spirits? What about gifts given by the Spirit for worship and praise—gifts like praying and singing in tongues? What about gifts that encourage people and build faith—exhortation, prophecy, miracles, the sharing of faith through testimony and Scripture?

To many modern Catholics, some of these gifts seem strange, impractical, and unnecessary. They may be listed in the New Testament, but they seem to have dropped out of the life of the church centuries ago—except for a few saints who possessed extraordinary charisms.

Furthermore, many Catholics think that there is really no place for these gifts in the official worship of the church, the liturgy. Praying in tongues, prophecy, and other spontaneous outbursts from the assembly—they view these as disorderly, subjective, probably emotional, and potentially divisive. It is to protect against these dangers and against possible confusion in worship that the church has a formal liturgy, they say.

It is undoubtedly true that the proper use and integration of these gifts of the Holy Spirit—including prophecy, prophetic glossolalia and its interpretation, praying and singing in tongues, testimony, exhortation, sharing Scripture and the like—pose the most difficult challenge today in churches with a rich liturgical life. Unfortunately, the solution that many churches have taken is simply to exclude or ignore these spiritual gifts, or at least to minimize their importance. This is fairly easy to do, since these gifts have not always been prominent in the everyday life of the church. Christians in the West, in particular, have a certain rationalistic prejudice against expressions of faith that are "suprarational"—that is, above reason—given by God to be accepted, used, and discerned spiritually rather than through reason alone.

This approach is ironic, because at the *heart* of Catholic liturgy is the Eucharist, which is certainly a suprarational mystery. Unaided human reason rejects the belief that the bread and wine of the Eucharist—which continue to taste, look, feel, and smell like bread and wine—actually become, in essence, the body, blood, soul, and divinity of Jesus Christ. How can anyone who believes in the real presence doubt that God can enable people to prophesy and to worship him in supernatural languages?

In an age that desires to reduce religion to that which is "reasonable" and that doubts God's very existence, is it surprising that God might restore some of the spiritual gifts for worship and praise that were signs of his presence in the primitive church? Once again, unbelievers need to see that God has broken into history in a radically new way in Jesus Christ and that he remains active and present in the world through the gifts, power, and guidance of the Holy Spirit. Perhaps even the church—which has the natural human tendency to encompass the mystery of faith in neat, predictable forms, in doctrinal definitions and set liturgical formulations—needs to be reminded occasionally of the sovereignty of God and of the need to respond more openly to the Holy Spirit, which "blows where it wills" (John 3:8). Many prominent leaders of the Catholic hierarchy have encouraged Catholics to be open to this "new" experience of the Spirit. Pope Benedict XVI, when he was a cardinal, wrote,

> In the heart of a world desiccated by rationalistic skepticism a new experience of the Holy Spirit has come about, amounting to a worldwide renewal movement. What the New Testament describes, with reference to the charisms, as a visible sign of the coming of the Spirit is no longer merely ancient, past history: this history is becoming a burning reality today.[11]

Pope Paul VI and Pope John Paul II also discerned the timeliness of the outpouring of the gifts and power of the Holy Spirit in the church today—signs of the "new Pentecost" for which Pope John XXIII prayed. They realized that the role of the office-holders, or hierarchy, of the church is not to quench the Spirit but to make room for him, finding ways for his work to become more public and prominent in the church's life.

This is what St. Paul had to do in dealing with the early Christian community in Corinth: find a way to correct the situation without quenching the Spirit. The Holy Spirit was lavishing his gifts upon the Corinthians, but these gifts were being misunderstood and sometimes abused. Rather than clamping down and prohibiting the use of spiritual gifts, however, Paul responded to the problem by *teaching*. First, he taught the church in Corinth about the value and meaning of the gifts of the Spirit, and then he gave detailed practical instruction about the gifts, including how to exercise them properly in the worship of the church. Paul wrote the Corinthians, "When you come together, each one has a hymn, a lesson, a revelation. . . . For God is not a God of confusion, but a God of peace" (1 Corinthians 14:26-33).

What could the church learn from St. Paul today, when God is again lavishing the Holy Spirit and his gifts upon his people? The first and most crucial lesson is for pastors to teach God's people the *meaning* and the *importance* of the gifts of the Holy Spirit. Of course, this requires that the pastors themselves have received this instruction. Catholics need to learn to be *open* to these gifts, even to seek them (see 1 Corinthians 14:1), and to accept them with gratitude.[12]

Catholics must hear that the gifts of the Holy Spirit are a normal part of the Christian life and are necessary for the life of the church. God never forces his gifts on anyone. If some members of the church decide that they do not wish to receive them (either through ignorance or indifference), then the Spirit will be quenched and the church will be impoverished.

Second, Catholic leaders must decide how the gifts of worship and praise are to be integrated into the worship of the church. They must teach their congregations how to use the gifts in worship, and then direct the process. This is what St. Paul did. But the approach taken by most dioceses and parishes has been insufficient. They have allowed a false understanding of the gifts of the Spirit to spread: that spiritual gifts are the concern of only a certain interest group in the church, the "charismatics." Some accommodation is made for them: the charismatics can have a special, nonliturgical meeting, where they can pray in tongues, prophesy, share testimony and Scripture, and exercise other gifts of the Holy Spirit. But this is not part of normal parish life. If there is a "new Pentecost" in the church, the impression is clearly given by most pastors that it is not for the whole church but just for a few "charismatics."

Integrating Charismatic Gifts into Parish Life

How can the gifts of the Holy Spirit be integrated into normal Catholic parish life? It must be acknowledged that there may be and will be *different* legitimate approaches here. One possible way to integrate them is to raise people's awareness gradually that each of them has been given gifts by the Holy Spirit to be used for serving God and others. Examples of the various gifts from Scripture could be presented and explained in a homily. Parishioners could be encouraged to think about their own gifts and to try to identify and use them in some way in their homes, in the parish, and in the world to make Christ present to others. If there is a charismatic prayer group in the parish or diocese, members of the parish could be *encouraged* to visit and participate to find out about a fuller life in the Holy Spirit, to see the gifts of the Holy Spirit being used to worship God and to build up a worshiping community. They could even be encouraged to pray for more of the presence and power of the Holy Spirit and his gifts in their lives.

A bold but desirable step would be to consider how the worship-related gifts of the Spirit could be integrated into the liturgy. Some areas have "charismatic" Masses, in which spiritual gifts are used at various points of the liturgy. These Masses give glory to God, are a powerful witness to those who come, and are a sort of testing ground for the church to learn how charisms can be integrated fruitfully into Catholic liturgy today.

For example, there might be a time toward the end of Mass (after holy Communion) for people to read a passage from Scripture, or to speak a prophecy or word from the Lord that they think is for the whole congregation. Also a "word of prayer" (members of the congregation praying or singing in tongues together) may be included in liturgically appropriate moments in the Mass. Some appropriate times for a word of prayer might be after the Gloria (a time set apart for praise and adoration) on Sundays; after the Great Amen, when the body and blood of Christ are elevated for adoration; and after reception of Communion, along with time for silent adoration and reflection.

This time of charismatic prayer need not be long—perhaps, only two or three minutes. But it would honor the Lord and (one would hope) edify the congregation. It would also encourage the use of the spiritual gifts and signify that they are truly a Catholic way of worshiping God—not something strange or "enthusiastic," not just for Pentecostal Christians or charismatics.

Of course, such a practice would need to be introduced properly and pastored sensitively, so that the whole parish or Catholic community would understand what was happening at the various points of the Mass. People who did not possess the gift of tongues or did not feel comfortable praying out loud, even in English, should be assured that it was fine not to. They could participate in this brief time of charismatic worship in any way they felt comfortable, such as in silent prayer.

Like all new things, this inclusion of a short time of charismatic prayer in the liturgy would be resisted by some Catholics. The assurance that this is fully biblical and Catholic and that no one is compelled to pray out loud would not allay all fear and objections. The parish would need courage to move ahead with this new direction. They would need the conviction that these worship gifts really are to be "received with gratitude" and are "exceedingly useful for the needs of the Church," as Vatican II teaches, and that there should be a way to express these gifts in the official worship of the church today, as there was in New Testament times. The intention is not to introduce something new or foreign to the liturgy but to recover and restore something very old and rich to the church's official worship.

To facilitate this process, the authors of *Fanning the Flame* offer some recommendations:

> Between Easter and Pentecost, both the newly baptized and all other parishioners can be led to savor the life in the Spirit through teachings on prayer, on receiving and using the charisms. Thus, prophecy, healing, discernment of spirits, prayer in tongues, and other charisms enter the normal flow of parish life, and have their place in daily parish activity (1 Corinthians 14). These spiritual gifts, intimately connected with the gift of the Spirit in initiation, will empower the many avenues of service through which parishioners will build up the communion which is the church.[13]

In particular, they see preparation for confirmation as an ideal time to teach openness to the Holy Spirit:

> We suggest that the intimate connection between confirmation and Christian initiation be stressed. For those who are already baptized, preparation for

confirmation would focus on renewal in the life of the Spirit, marked by personal conversion to Christ, and openness to the person and the gifts of the Holy Spirit. Thus, confirmation, as currently practiced, could enable a renewal of Christian initiation. Ideally, preparation for confirmation would be incorporated into the parish preparation for Easter, along with the RCIA.[14]

Another way to enrich the liturgy would be to use the praise-filled music that emerged through the anointing and renewal of the Holy Spirit in the church. The songs and hymns adapted should be musically rich and theologically sound.

Many of these songs are direct expressions of biblical passages and themes, as has been encouraged by Vatican II.[15] Unfortunately, the producers of most parish Mass books and other community and liturgical materials have drawn upon very little of the best music that has emerged from charismatic renewal in the Catholic Church. This is tragic, considering that one of the most evident contributions of this movement of the Holy Spirit has been the revitalization of communal praise and worship, expressed particularly in its music.

The fact that this rich and abundant contribution has been largely ignored and minimally represented in the liturgical resources used by most parishes is another symptom of the basic problem: the gifts and graces that have come to the Catholic Church through charismatic renewal have been viewed as something for a particular group, and not for the benefit and use of the entire church. I strongly agree with the vision of the Catholic scholars who wrote in 1990,

In our vision, a renewed parish is a community worshiping in vibrant liturgy, bonded together by the Holy Spirit, serving one another, committed to ongoing conversion and growth, reaching out to the inactive, the unchurched and to the poor. Such parishes confront us with the gospel and evangelize our culture. In these communities, as in the Acts of the Apostles and the early church, the charisms of the Holy Spirit are identified and welcomed.[16]

The positive side, though, is that God is graciously blessing the church in our day with an abundance of gifts of the Holy Spirit, of all varieties, for the strengthening of the people and as a witness to the world. All God asks of all of us is to desire his gifts, to be open to whatever blessings he gives us, and to find ways to express the gifts of the Holy Spirit in the life and worship of the church. God's gifts are, after all, for his glory. The thanks that we can offer to God for the gifts of the Holy Spirit is to accept them and to use them with diligence and freedom to serve the Lord and our neighbor.

Notes

Introduction (pp. 8–12)

1. Cyril of Jerusalem, from *Catechesis,* quoted in *The Liturgy of the Hours,* Vol. 2 (New York: Catholic Book Publishing Co., 1975), 561.

2. John Paul II, *Tertio Millennio Adveniente* (As the Third Millennium Draws Near), Nov. 10, 1994, 1.

3. John Paul II, *Tertio Millennio Adveniente,* 44, 45. See also John Paul II's encyclical letter *Dominum et Vivificantem* (Lord and Giver of Life), May 18, 1986, 51.

Chapter One: Who Is the Holy Spirit? (pp. 13–23)

1. These references are summarized in "The Name, Titles, and Symbols of the Holy Spirit" in *Catechism of the Catholic Church* (Washington, DC: United States Catholic Conference—*Libreria Editrice Vaticana,* 1994), 182–85, nos. 691–701. Hereafter references to this work will be indicated with a parenthetical notation of the paragraph number, such as (691–701).

2. New American Bible, footnote on John 14:16.

3. The phrase "and the Son" (*filioque*) was added later by the Catholic Church, following the theology of St. Augustine in his profound treatise *On the Trinity.* It has been a source of dispute between Catholic and Orthodox Christians.

4. Cyril of Jerusalem, Catechetical Lecture 16 "On the Holy Spirit" in *The Liturgy of the Hours,* Vol. 2 (New York: Catholic Book Publishing Co., 1975), 967–68.

5. Through the Spirit, Jesus' promise is fulfilled: "If a man loves me, he will keep my word, and my Father will love him, and we will come to him and make our home with him" (John 14:23). Since the persons of God are perfectly one and insepa-

rable, through the Holy Spirit the fullness of God—Father, Son, and Spirit—comes to us and dwells within us.

Chapter Two: The Importance of Pentecost (pp. 24–40)

1. Second Vatican Council, *Lumen Gentium* (Dogmatic Constitution on the Church), 13.
2. Henry Chadwick, *The Early Church* (Baltimore, MD: Penguin, 1967), p. 54.
3. Chadwick, p. 56.
4. Chadwick, pp. 56, 57.

Chapter Three: The Holy Spirit and Prayer (pp. 41–58)

1. Thomas Merton, *The Wisdom of the Desert* (New York: New Directions, 1960), p. 50.
2. Sometimes the Holy Spirit is called the "Spirit of God" (Matthew 3:16; 12:28; Romans 8:9, 14; 15:19; 1 Corinthians 2:11, 12, 14; 3:16; 6:11; 7:40; 12:3; 2 Corinthians 3:3; 1 John 4:2); sometimes, the "Spirit of Christ" (Romans 8:9; Galatians 4:6; Philippians 1:19; 1 Peter 1:11). Jesus sometimes speaks of the Holy Spirit as someone he will send to the church from the Father (John 15:26); at other times, he speaks of the Spirit as a gift sent by the Father (see Luke 11:13) or "whom the Father will send in my name" (John 14:17), or as the "promise of my Father" (Luke 24:49).
3. As a sign of this, even when Mary visited her cousin Elizabeth with Jesus in her womb, the babe in Elizabeth's womb leapt, and Elizabeth "was filled with the Holy Spirit, and she proclaimed with a loud cry, 'Blessed are you among women, and blessed is the fruit of your womb!'" (Luke 1:39-42).
4. John Paul II, *Tertio Millennio Adveniente* (As the Third Millennium Draws Near), Nov. 10, 1994, 8.
5. St. Augustine, from Sermon 13 "On the Season," quoted

in *The Liturgy of the Hours,* Vol. 1 (New York: Catholic Book Publishing Co., 1975), 541.

6. Didymus of Alexandria, "On the Trinity," (Lib. 2, 12: pg 39: 667–674), quoted in *The Liturgy of the Hours,* Vol. 2 (New York: Catholic Book Publishing Co., 1975), 882–83.

7. Second Vatican Council, *Sacrosanctum Concilium* (Constitution on the Sacred Liturgy), 10, Abbot translation.

8. John Paul II, *Crossing the Threshold of Hope* (New York: Alfred A. Knopf, 1994), pp. 17–18.

9. John Paul II, *Crossing the Threshold of Hope,* p. 19.

Chapter Four: The Spirit of Truth (pp. 59–79)

1. St. Vincent of Lerins, from *First Instruction,* quoted in *The Liturgy of the Hours,* Vol. 4 (New York: Catholic Book Publishing Co., 1975), 363–64.

2. John Henry Newman, *An Essay in Aid of a Grammar of Assent,* I. T. Ker, ed. (Oxford: Clarendon, 1985), 57.

3. Newman, 60.

4. Newman, 102.

5. Second Vatican Council, *Dei Verbum* (Dogmatic Constitution on Divine Revelation), 5.

6. Second Vatican Council, *Dei Verbum,* 5.

7. Teresa of Avila, *The Way of Perfection,* trans. and ed. by E. Allison Peers, (Garden City, NY: Doubleday Image Books, 1964), pp. 62, 63.

Chapter Five: The Spirit of Holiness (pp. 80–98)

1. Theophilus of Antioch, from the book addressed to Autolycus, quoted in *The Liturgy of the Hours,* Vol. 2 (New York: Catholic Book Publishing Co., 1975), 241.

2. Theophilus, 241.

3. Note that the prophets, and later Jesus, clarified that

each person would be punished for his own sin, not for the sins of his father (see Jeremiah 31:29-30; Ezekiel 18:1-4; John 9:1-3).

4. John Paul II, *Dominum et Vivificantem* (Lord and Giver of Life), May 18, 1986, 55.

5. Second Vatican Council, *Lumen Gentium* (Dogmatic Constitution on the Church), 40.

6. John Paul II, *Christifideles Laici* (The Lay Members of Christ's Faithful People), December 30, 1988. All quotes in this section are from no. 16.

7. John Paul II, *Dominum et Vivificantem*, 31.

8. *Dominum et Vivificantem*, 46.

9. *Dominum et Vivificantem*. 47.

10. *Dominum et Vivificantem*, 47.

Chapter Six: Evangelization: Where's the Power? (pp. 99–117)

1. Roland Allen, *The Spontaneous Expansion of the Church* (Grand Rapids, MI: Eerdmans, 1962), p. 9.

2. Paul VI, *Evangelii Nuntiandi* (On Evangelization in the Modern World), Dec. 8, 1975, 75.

3. Paul VI, 75.

4. Second Vatican Council, *Ad Gentes Divinitus* (Decree on the Church's Missionary Activity), 2.

5. John Paul II, *Redemptoris Missio* (Mission of the Redeemer), Dec. 7, 1990, 2.

6. John Paul II, *Redemptoris Missio,* 2.

7. John Paul II, 46, 47.

8. John Paul II, 24.

9. John Paul II, 46.

10. John Paul II, 26.

11. John Paul II, 26.

12. Paul VI, 75.

13. Paul VI, 75.

14. Peter Kreeft, *Fundamentals of the Faith* (San Francisco: Ignatius Press, 1988), p. 142.

15. Allen, pp. 12, 50.

16. John Paul II, 87.

17. These characteristics are mentioned in *Redemptoris Missio,* nos. 88–91.

18. Paul VI, 76.

19. Paul VI, 77.

20. Paul VI, 80.

Chapter Seven: Building the Church (pp. 118–42)

1. George Montague and Kilian McDonnell, *Fanning the Flame* (Collegeville, MN: Liturgical Press, 1991), pp. 14–15.

2. Second Vatican Council, *Lumen Gentium* (Dogmatic Constitution on the Church), 36.

3. John Paul II, *Christifideles Laici* (The Lay Members of Christ's Faithful People), December 30, 1988, 24.

4. Second Vatican Council, *Lumen Gentium,* 12; See also Second Vatican Council, *Apostolicam Actuositatem* (Decree on the Apostolate of the Laity), 3, and John Paul II in *L'Osservatore Romano,* July 1, 1992, English edition, 1.

5. Karl Rahner, "Observations on the Factor of the Charismatic in the Church," in *Theological Investigations,* Vol. 12 (New York: Seabury, 1974), p. 83.

6. Second Vatican Council, *Lumen Gentium,* 12; *Apostolicam Actuositatem,* 3.

7. Joseph Ratzinger with Vittorio Messori, *The Ratzinger Report* (San Francisco: Ignatius, 1985), 44.

8. Karl Rahner, "The Church of the Saints," in *Theological Investigations,* Vol. 3, pp. 103, 104.

9. Rahner, "Observations on the Factor of the Charismatic in the Church," Vol. 12, p. 84.

10. Paul VI, Address to Synod of Bishops, Oct. 10, 1974, quoted in Kilian McDonnell, ed., *Open the Windows* (South Bend, IN: Greenlawn Press, 1989), pp. 7–8.

11. John Paul II, Audience with Italian Charismatic Renewal, Nov. 23, 1980, quoted in *Open the Windows,* pp. 31–32.

12. John Paul II, Audience, pp. 31–32.

13. John Paul II, *L'Osservatore Romano,* July 1, 1992, English edition, 11.

14. Paul VI, quoted in *Open the Windows,* pp. 14, 15.

15. Second Vatican Council, *Lumen Gentium,* 12; *Apostolicam Actuositatem,* 3; *Catechism,* 798–801.

Chapter Eight: The Spirit as Guarantee of our Inheritance (pp. 143–56)

1. C. L. Mitton, "Paul's Certainties: The Gift of the Spirit and Life beyond Death—2 Corinthians v. 1–5," *Expository Times* 69:4 (1958), p. 262.

2. Mitton, p. 262.

3. Mitton, p. 263.

4. Pedro Saenz de Argandona, "The Spiritual Gospel of John," *Homiletic and Pastoral Review,* April 1994, p. 51.

5. William Sanday, *The Epistle to the Romans* (New York: Scribner's, 1869), p. 209.

6. C. Clarke Oke, "A Suggestion with Regard to Romans 8:23," abg. by J. Harold Greenle, *Bible Translator,* 11 (1960), p. 91.

7. J. D. G. Dunn, "1 Corinthians 15:45—Last Adam, Life-giving Spirit," in *Christ and Spirit in the New Testament,* Lindars and Smalley, eds. (Cambridge: University Press, 1973), p. 138.

8. Rudolph Schnackenburg, *Baptism in the Thought of St. Paul,* trans. G.R. Beasley-Murray (New York: Herder and Herder, 1964), p. 88.

9. A. M. Hunter, *Paul and His Predecessors* (Philadelphia: Westminister Press, 1961), p. 61.

10. Hunter, p. 70.

Chapter Nine: Unity: The Spirit's Greatest Gift (pp. 157–82)

1. John Paul II, "Christian Unity Is Gift of the Spirit," *L'Osservatore Romano,* January 27, 1993, English edition, 11.

2. Günther Bornkamm, *Paul,* trans. D. M. G. Stalker (New York: Harper and Row, 1971), p. 181.

3. John Paul II, "Christian Unity," 11.

4. Second Vatican Council, *Unitatis Redintegratio* (Decree on Ecumenism), 1.

5. Second Vatican Council, *Unitatis Redintegratio,* 24.

6. Paul VI, Address to First International Catholic Charismatic Leaders' Conference, 1973, quoted in Kilian McDonnell, ed., *Open the Windows* (South Bend, IN: Greenlawn Press, 1989), pp. 4, 5.

Chapter Ten: The Spouse of the Holy Spirit (pp. 183–203)

1. Theological reflection and the liturgy have, in fact, noted that the sanctifying intervention of the Spirit in Mary was a culminating moment of the Spirit's action in the history of salvation. Thus, for example, some fathers and writers of the church attributed Mary's original holiness to the work of the Spirit. Examining more deeply the mystery of the incarnation, they saw in the mysterious relationship between the Spirit and Mary an aspect redolent of marriage, poetically portrayed by Prudentius: "The unwed Virgin espoused the Spirit," and they called her the "Temple of the Holy Spirit," an expression that emphasizes the sacred character of the Virgin, now the permanent dwelling of the Spirit of God.

2. Bertrand Buby, "Mary in Prayer," in *Mary, the Spirit,*

and the Church, Vincent P. Branick, ed. (Ramsey, NJ: Paulist, 1980), pp. 94, 95.

3. John Paul II, *Redemptoris Mater* (Mother of the Redeemer), Mar. 25, 1987, 24.

4. René Laurentin, "Mary: Model of the Charismatic as Seen in Acts 1–2, Luke 1–2, and John," in *Mary, the Spirit, and the Church,* p. 37. Fr. Laurentin also concludes that Mary exercised the charism of glossolalia:

"To say that Mary exercised the gift of glossolalia—that she participated in this collective chant of the first Pentecost, is not novel. It was the commonly held opinion in classical mariology, from the pseudo-Albert in the thirteenth century to the Roman mariologist G. Roschini, who died in 1977. . . .The connection between the charism of glossolalia and the prophecy of the Magnificat is clear in the very words used by Luke. The word Magnificat (Greek *megalunei*) which is the first word of this canticle, characterizes glossolalia, according to Acts 10:46. "They spoke in tongues and magnified God" [cf. Acts 19:17]. This can be compared with Acts 19:10 which speaks of prophecy and glossolalia. The word megaleia characterizes the glossolalia of Pentecost in Acts 2:11" (Laurentin, p. 38).

5. Paul VI, *Marialis Cultus* (Devotion to the Blessed Virgin Mary), Feb. 2, 1974, 26.

6. Frederick M. Jelly, "Mary and the Gifts and Charisms of the Holy Spirit," in *Mary, the Spirit, and the Church,* pp. 88–89. Fr. Jelly also beautifully sums up the work of the Spirit in Mary's life on these pages:

No matter what may be the perspective or vantage point from which we view Mary as the flesh and blood icon of the Holy Spirit, we behold the completely charismatic Christian, who like her Son always accepted divine gifts and charisms for the sake of others. . . . Perfected in her own spiritual life by the gifts of wisdom, knowledge and understanding, Mary was ever prepared to bring Christ to others. In the Spirit, contemplating him in her heart over and over again, she was always ready to show him to visitors, whether they be the Jewish shepherds or the gentile Magi. Mary is the mother of good counsel, telling us over and over again as she did the servants at the wedding feast of Cana: "Do whatever he tells you" (John 2:5). Filled with the gift of fortitude she journeyed through life on her "pilgrimage of faith," as Vatican II describes it (*Lumen Gentium, 58*) right to the foot of the cross, where she received the charism of becoming the spiritual mother of us all. Who can plumb the depths of her piety and of her reverential loving fear of the Lord, when in her compassion she courageously offered her Son back to the Father in the Spirit?

7. Laurentin, p. 34. Fr. Laurentin also explains why only the gift of glossolalia was given at Pentecost, and what it meant:

"It may seem surprising that in this account of the first Pentecost, Luke mentions only the charism of glossolalia, whereas for the Pentecost of John the Baptist's disciples at Ephesus, he mentions two charisms, "The Holy Spirit came on them, and they began to speak in tongues and to prophesy" (Acts 19:6).

"This restriction is for symbolic reasons:

"A. Jewish tradition presented the feast of Pentecost [the feast of the Sinai Covenant] as the anti-Babel, the transcending of the confusion and divisions symbolized by the barrier which languages erect between peoples. It is this communication barrier that is transcended by the gift of "new tongues" as the Pentecost narrative puts it [Acts 2:4]: in short, the gift of an angelic language, which is a language of praise, a language for God, transcending logical, rational speech, recreates the unity of mankind, setting forth once again on the march toward God.

"B. This choice of Luke is due also to the fact that glossolalia was a striking experience for two reasons: exteriorly, for the witnesses, who react in different ways [Acts 2:7-13], and interiorly, because it is the catalyzing sign of a liberation, still living on today" (Laurentin, pp. 34–35).

8. Laurentin, pp. 33–34.

9. A life baptized in the Spirit is marked both by an experience of dynamic union with God and by an experience of charisms given by the Spirit. These enable us to serve God in praise and worship, to serve one another in love by prophecy, healing and other gifts, and to empower our participation in the church's ministry in society. These charisms belong to the church today. According to Karl Rahner, prophecy is "a permanent endowment of the church and a proof of her supernatural mission." Karl Rahner and H. Vorgrimler say that charisms "like office and sacraments belong to the nature of the church . . . the forms taken by *charismata* . . . cannot be foreseen, precisely because they belong by their very nature to the saving history of the church; and therefore they must be constantly rediscovered and accepted." The recovery of the baptism in the Spirit and the charisms is needed in all the institutions of the church (George Montague and Kilian McDonnell, *Fanning the Flame* (Collegeville, MN: Liturgical Press, 1991), pp. 22–23).

10. Laurentin, p. 34.

11. Paul VI, quoted in *L'Osservatore Romano*, Dec. 7, 1972, English edition, in Edward D. O'Connor, *Pope Paul and the Spirit* (Notre Dame, IN: Ave Maria, 1978), p. 184.

12. Maximilian Kolbe, Conference of April 9, 1938 and Conference of February 5, 1941, quoted in H. M. Manteau-Bonamy, *Immaculate Conception and the Holy Spirit* (Libertyville, IL: Prow Books/Franciscan Marytown Press, 1977), pp. 49, 50, 52

13. Manteau-Bonamy, pp. 50–51.

14. *Lumen Gentium,* 53, (Manteau-Bonamy's translation).

15. Manteau-Bonamy, p. 51.

Appendix: "Spirit-Filled" Worship in the Catholic Tradition (pp. 204–20)

1. Tertullian, "On Baptism," as quoted in Kilian McDonnell, and George T. Montague, *Christian Initiation and Baptism in the*

Holy Spirit (Collegeville, MN: Liturgical Press, 1991), p. 98.

2. McDonnell and Montague, p. 99.

3. Origen, "On Prayer," in *Origen: Selected Writings*, trans. Rowan A. Greer, (New York: Paulist, 1979), pp. 164–65.

4. Eddie Ensley, *Sounds of Wonder: A Popular History of Speaking in Tongues in the Catholic Tradition* (New York: Paulist, 1977), pp. 3, 4. It is clear that the church fathers regarded wordless prayer and singing as a natural human activity and saw a strong identity between the spiritual jubilation of Christians and natural human jubilation.

5. Augustine, from Sermon on Psalm 32, quoted in *The Liturgy of the Hours*, Vol. 4 (New York: Catholic Book Publishing Co., 1975), 1576–77.

6. Joseph Ratzinger with Vittorio Messori, *The Ratzinger Report* (San Francisco: Ignatius, 1985), 126.

7. Second Vatican Council, *Sacrosanctum Concilium* (Constitution on the Sacred Liturgy), Abbot translation, 14. See also *Catechism*, 1140–41.

8. Second Vatican Council, *Sacrosanctum Concilium*, 19.

9. *Sacrosanctum Concilium*, 21.

10. *Sacrosanctum Concilium*, 22.

11. Ratzinger, 151.

12. Second Vatican Council, *Lumen Gentium* (Dogmatic Constitution on the Church), 12.

13. George Montague and Kilian McDonnell, *Fanning the Flame* (Collegeville, MN: Liturgical Press, 1991), p. 24.

14. Montague and McDonnell, *Fanning the Flame*, p. 25.

15. See *Sacrosanctum Concilium*, chapter six, and *Dei Verbum*, chapter six.

16. Montague and McDonnell, *Fanning the Flame*, p. 23.